From the

Sma' Lines and the Creels

to the

Seine Net and the Prawns

A Study of the Inshore Fishing Industry around
the East Coast of Fife

from

St. Andrews to Buckhaven

by

Peter Smith

of

Cellardyke

D1470790

From the

Sma' Lines and the Creels

to the

Seine Net and the Prawns

A Study of the Inshore Fishing Industry around
the East Coast of Fife

from

St. Andrews to Buckhaven

by

Peter Smith of Cellardyke

Published by:
James Corstorphine
45 Hawthorn Street
Leven, Fife KY8 4QE

Website: http://members.tripod.com/~corstorphine/oakville.html

Printed in Scotland by Levenmouth Printers

ISBN 0-9525621-3-8

Two old masters with 'The jib tae the Borak'. At the helm of ML67 *Janet* is T.Anderson, former master of three boats all named *Carmi*, the last one being a Steam Drifter. At his side is Martin Gardner, former master of three vessels named *Vanguard*, again the last a Steam Drifter. Martin Gardner was also a former Coxwain of one of the Anstruther sailing lifeboats.

Contents

St Rule's Tower dominates this view of the Inner Harbour at St Andrews
(from the Cowie Collection, St Andrews University Library)

St Andrews

St. Andrews by the Northern Sea
A haunted town it is to me
A little city worn and grey
The grey north ocean girds it round
and o'er the rocks and up the bay
The long sea rollers surge and sound
and still the thin and biting spray
Drives down the melancholy street
And still endure and still decay
Towers that the salt winds vainly beat
Ghost like and shadowy they stand
Dim mirrored in the wet sea sand.

So goes the poem by Andrew Lang, named Almae Matres after St. Andrews and Oxford. The poem was written around the 1860's. In my youth I heard the Gifford lecture on Andrew Lang and the Scottish Borders in Lower College Hall, St Andrews, given by John Buchan, before the Chairman, Sir. James C. Irvine, the Principal and an audience so tightly packed that they were seated on the floor in the passageway.

It was about this time that John Buchan wrote a book *The Free Fishers,* which begins with a St. Andrews University Professor walking back from Pittenweem to St. Andrews during the night, having been at a seaman's Secret Society meeting in Pittenweem. This book was badly received in the other side of the Forth as they really did have a Society of Free Fishers at Newhaven. It is but a few years since the society was wound up and among the names of the society members which appeared in the 1951 publication *The Society of Free Fishermen of Newhaven* were Wilson and Ramsay, whose descendants were among the top fishermen among the ring net men of the Firth of Forth. I was friendly with G. Wilson of the Leith registered boat *Gratitude* and Robbie Ramsay of the *Endeavour*. The latter was a close enough friend to give me hints about the fishing. Their own craft did not exceed 50 ft. and it is of this size of boat and under, and their crews, that this book is mainly about.

Having mentioned St. Andrews first, I will begin here and work around the east coast of Fife, finishing at Buckhaven. I looked up the *First Statistical Account 1791-99*, and it is sad to read the history of the St Andrews fisher folk. In the account, there appears an appendix to the history of the fishers, dated 1765, the details of which I will recount here, although I have shortened it as far as possible:

"The morning was quiet and all the boats had shot their lines. About 7 a.m. they saw bad weather coming from the north-east and when the storm struck each boat made for the nearest beach. Two of the boats which were near each other had got so close to the East Sands that the people on the beach began to wade into the water in order to assist their friends. Suddenly, one boat raised on the top of a prodigious wave and was driven over the head of the other. The uppermost boat was instantly either buried in the sand, or carried back by the reflux, and no part of it's crew was ever again seen. The undermost boat was drawn ashore by the crowd with all its occupants alive".

The writer of the account stated that he had seen and felt the wound made in the head of a boy in the stern of the undermost boat by the keel of the uppermost. On this occasion, out of a total of five boats, three were totally lost and the other two were damaged and most of the tackle lost. Twelve men were lost, of whom only one was unmarried, leaving twenty-eight children without a father. A subscription was made for the bereaved, which raised £317.

And so, for several years, there were no fishermen in St. Andrews until, in 1803, two fisher families were brought from Shetland of whom one remained and the other returned north. I will now quote George Bruce:

"for this year 1882 there are no fewer than 24 large deep sea going boats over 50 ft. keel each worth over £300 with their gear. As well as a dozen half decked boats and another dozen small yawls engaged in the crab and hand line fishing employing about 200 men, against a score in 1803".

He mentions the building of three large boats during the previous year, 1881. The *Sea King, Our Queen* and *Fisher Lassie*, the latter being 53 ft. long, were carvel built at either Cellardyke or St. Monans. There is an interesting paragraph in Bruce's book about *Our Queen*. Instead of being lug sailed, she was rigged fore and aft and, what impressed me more, she had a safety rail or bulwark built around the gunwales at knee height, giving the deck a feeling of security. It is a pity it didn't appear to catch on, as I'm sure it would have saved many lives.

Incidentally, I have checked the DE (Dundee) registered fishing boats for 1914, and there was a *Fisher Lassie* DE 176, owned by R. Gordon. I also have a list of the last St. Andrews fishing boats to go to the Drave, and they were *Theodosia* DE22, *Catherine Black* DE 175, *Fisher Lassie* DE 176, and *Nil Desperanda* DE 39.

I've been told it is unwise to quote Bruce, but that smack rigged boat certainly intrigued me, as I was brought up with the lug sail. Walking down to Anster Harbour with my father, I would shudder going along West Forth Street in Cellardyke when we passed the only trees in the street if the wind could be heard whistling in the branches. My father would say, "It'll be neck or nothing the day. Twa rings tae the stellum". The stellum was an eye bolt for securing the bottom of the active part of the sail, near the foot of the mast, beside what was known as the fore thaft. You will see the word 'stellum' on page 270 in Bruce's book on St. Andrews Bay and I haven't seen it written anywhere else. Around 1840 there were 6 or 7 yawls of about 28 ft keel length in St Andrews and, until 1842 when Playfair became Provost, the fishermen got their bait free of charge. After a long series of statements, they were charged 6/- per cwt. cart load of mussels (18 heavy baskets) or 4d. per basket. From 4d. the price was raised to 6d., then 9d., then 1/-, then 2/-.

Before giving details of the St Andrews fleet, I will quote from the First Statistical Account and Bruce's Statistical Account. The First Statistical Account refers to 'the flat sandy bay abounding with large flounders, cockles and mussels':

The gatherers, after gathering the mussels from the Eden for two miles, sell them in St. Andrews at 2d. the measured peck. The mussels are used by the

9

fishermen as bait for the haddock. St. Andrews Bay until the last few years abounded in haddock, which sold to St. Andrews and Cupar and the north side of Fife as far as 10 miles. These haddocks were of a smaller size than those of the Firth of Forth, but of a better flavour in the opinion of these people of this place. The shallow water over a sandy bottom, affords great plenty of flat fish such as flounders, sole, skate, halibut, turbot and in deeper water, ling and larger cod, the latter sold at 2d or 3d. per lb. Since the departure of the haddock, the fishermen have become poor and storms which raise tremendous seas have destroyed their lives".

I will close this first chapter with an extract from Bruce in 1882 depicting better times for the future:

"Each man generally has 14 strings of haddock lines 140 yards long with 115 hooks on each string, thus a boat's crew of 7 men have 13,720 yards (nearly 8 miles) with 11,270 hooks. When the weather is favourable, the St. Andrews boats will land each day on the old pier at least £100 worth of fish, little short of £20,000 per year".

'Bully' Tam Wilson redding lines at St Andrews Pier c.1935 (Cowie Collection)

10

St Andrews Harbour in 1900. The fishing boat belonged to local man J.Melville
(Cowie Collection)

Local fishermen in the ancient fishing quarter of St Andrews, c.1910 (Cowie Collection)

Fishermen's houses at the rear of the 'Royal George', St Andrews, c.1910
(Cowie Collection)

St Andrews Harbour c.1905 (Cowie Collection)

12

Student Days

Researching the history of the St Andrews fishing fleet and writing down the boats' names and owners brings to mind my first year at St Andrews University in the 1930's. My father had a half share in a 30ft motor yawl with James Watson (Patchie), in which they went to the sproules, haurlins and sma' lines. She had an 'Atlantic' engine of about 30 H.P., whereas comparable vessels in the Pittenweem fleet had 30 H.P. Kelvin engines. She was a good yawl, but the 'Atlantic' engine gave trouble, so they were glad to sell her on at a profit. Patchie then borrowed the motor yawl *Day Dawn* from his brother-in-law Peter Waters of St. Andrews. She had a 15 H.P. Kelvin engine, and Patchie went to sea in her for the rest of his active life. My father went in her occasionally as part of the winter herring crew as Patchie only used one of the crew during the summer. It was at this time that Patchie came to me and said "I hear you're gaun to the University. I tell't Peter Waters and you're to gan and see him". Well, I was somewhat shy and overwhelmed with the newness of the University, so I was pleased to have someone living locally to visit. I lived down in Abbey Street, near the Crown Hotel, and I soon spotted Peter Waters. Incidentally, you can see his photograph in Bobby Burnet's book *The St. Andrews Opens*, page 107, when he was caddie to Bobby Locke. Peter wouldn't travel, however, so Bobby Locke got another caddie. Peter was to caddie once again in 1946 when Snead won the Championship. When I met Peter sometime later, I remarked "I saw ye caddying to Bobby Locke, Peter, how did ye get on wi' him". Peter replied "If Bobby Locke had done what I tell't him at the 14th., he would have been Open Champion the day". Well history decreed otherwise. I saw the greatest hitter of a gowf ba' in Snead that I have ever seen, not the best putter.

Peter was a pretty independent character and he was the Janitor to the wee school behind the Cathedral. He lived in the pend halfway down North Castle Street, where I went to see his wife, Patchie's sister. She was as wee as Patchie and I got a great welcome because I was like her, a Dyker. This was a most fortuitous introduction for me as through him I met the four

Chisholm brothers, who were well known golf caddies. It was through the Chisholms and their compatriots that I came to be enlightened about the Royal and Ancient game. Only one, James 'Tip' Anderson, is left of those caddies I came to know. Three of the Chisholm brothers were fishermen caddies.

I was lonely in my first year at the University as I had no money. It's no place for a poor man's son and I found myself gravitating to the harbour, where I helped to tie rapes on the nets for one of the Chisholms at winter herring time. One night, his crew man didn't turn up, so he asked me if I would go with him. Being young and foolhardy, I said "Yes". His boat was an 18 ft. sailing yawl, named the *Sunbeam*.

"Since you're a Dyker", says he, "you can steer." "Gladly" says I, for I knew I would be less nervous with something to do. So we sped down the coast towards Kingsbarns as the herring were in the Haikes, which stretched from Kingsbarns to Fife Ness. We shot the nets to the north side of Kingsbarns, being afraid of the Dykers, St. Monancers and ring net boats. It was somewhat primitive as I noticed that instead of a bow (buoy) to keep the nets vertical, a 2 gallon petrol tin was used, empty of course. We sailed back to St. Andrews a much lighter yawl, without our cargo of nets and anchors. Despite the lightness of the vessel, the skipper insisted on full sail with the tack 'forrit' instead of 'at the stellum'. Well we survived, thanks I may say to my upbringing and experience.

"Sit on the weather side o' the tully", my Uncle Dave said, "and loaf when you see a flan (squall) coming". The Dykers said 'loaf' when you put the boat's head into the wind and 'hardup' when away from the wind.

He was a pretty tough guy. They said he had been out in Canada for a while. He said to me when we got in to the harbour, "will ye manage the morn's mornin'?" "Oh no", I said, "this is the only suit I possess".

He got herrin' the following morning as I had a look down from the head of the brae before I went to my first class and I could see all the St. Andrews yawls had herrin'. I kept clear of him for a while after that, but I once heard him raging over yankee amateurs as he caddied on the Old course.

The next one, Willie Chisholm, you'll see in *Shadows of St. Andrews*

Past, page 27, as well as 'Sand Shoes' (Sandy), the youngest and best natured of the brothers.

I think we sold both a yawl and a dinghy to Willie and, whether my father realised it or not, Willie could be somewhat difficult to deal with. As father grew older, he missed going to the creels during the summer and said that he was vexed that he had sold his yawl, so I said to him, "Let's go up and see the Chisholms. They always have dinghies for hire during the summer and if it's only a few creels you want to play with, you've got some creels up the loft. We'll easily knock up another dozen".

So we went up to St Andrews, where we found Willie at the harbour. I left father talking to Willie after he pointed out seven or eight dinghies that he owned. I went across the wee bridge and walked around the boats which were lying near the East Bents putting green, where they had been hauled up for the Winter. When Willie and my father weren't looking, I took a coin and scratched under the gunwale on the port side of the fore thaft. After they had bargained away (which they both enjoyed), they agreed a price, which I had to pay. I pointed out the boat we would be taking. I intended to use one of Alex Myles of Cellardyke's fleet of lorries to take the boat back to Anster, so I said "Eck Myles' lorry will be up some day soon for this dinghy, Willie. I see you smile. If we don't get this one, the one you send will be returned. Before you boys arrived I put a mark on it and I alone know where the mark is". Willie's smile vanished and we got the dinghy we wanted!

I went with father to the creels each summer until 1947, a year when I never saw clearer water for a long way off shore. The sea was so calm and still that when a departing steam drifter disturbed the sand at the harbour mouth, it settled on top of the tangles about the Hannah Harvey lighthouse, where it remained for more than a week with a dead tide and still air. By the way, they used to say you can't catch lobsters in clear water. My father never fished better and I was reluctant to leave him to go back to teaching mathematics at the end of the school holidays.

When he retired we sold the dinghy and creels back to Willie, and he and I loaded it onto the lorry at the slipway opposite the Co-op shop to be taken back to St Andrews.

That leaves Sandy Chisholm, the youngest. I liked him best and, when there was a golf competition in progress on the Old Course which closed the road completely in front of Tom Morris's shop, they had a five barred gate across. I wasn't going to pay full fare to get in after the school came out and, as Sandy was often in charge of opening and shutting that gate, we just waited on a nod from 'Sand Shoes' and we were in! He was still caddying in 1971 when Great Britain and Ireland won the Walker Cup and was the first to tip me off that we had a chance. "Ask Tip" he said and 'Tip' agreed. And so a great final night was enjoyed by those of us who had endured so many defeats. I may say I was present as a student at the previous victory in 1938.

The Inner Harbour at St Andrews in the early 1900's (Cowie Collection)

'Poetry Peter' Smith, the Author's father, at the 'Sproules'

Crail and Cellardyke

A sproul, a lead, a guid hand line,
The "May" - jist ony day it's fine.

(from 'Tae Jeems', by 'Poetry Peter' Smith, the Author's Father)

Sproul, Sproule, Spruell, Sprol and Sprole are various different spellings for the artificial fish used on hand lines, which were made from white metal, sometimes lead. The sproul was given a scrape with a knife on the way to the fishing grounds, the objective being to have a shining artificial fish to attract the cod, which were then caught by the hook that was attached to the device. Once the lines had been lowered, they were jerked up and down in order to make the sproul dance around in the water. If one of the crew caught a big fish, one of the other crew members helped him haul it aboard using the 'clip', a wooden stick with a great big hook made fast to the end. As the fish approached the surface, he used the clip to hook the cod anywhere on its body before hauling it over the gunwale and on to the boat's deck.

If you wish to see any of these old hand lines and sproules, ask at the Scottish Fisheries Museum in Anstruther. If they are not on show, they may be seen on request.

One Saturday morning in the 1930's I was on my way to Anster harbour from my house in West Forth Street, Cellardyke, when I met a man I knew, Tam Lowrie. Tam was a crew member of the steam drifter *Violet*, and was on his way home from a fishing trip. I remarked on the large cod he was carrying and he told me that at the end of his watch the boat's skipper, who had the last watch before dawn, said "you neednae go back to your bed. I'll gie them half an hour, then we'll haul".

In order to pass the time before the drift nets were hauled, Tam decided to try a spot of fishing on his own. "I aye keep a sproul in the sma' boat, so I gied it a bit scrape", said Tam "and then it wis ower the side. We would be aff Fife Ness, where the ebb tide had taken us. I wasnae long doon when I got him, and there he is."

I remember Tam Lowrie because his father was one of the St. Monans men lost in the Wash in the terrible storm of 1875 on their passage home from Yarmouth. Two Cellardyke boats and three St. Monans boats were lost with all hands, a total of 37 men. His father was in the St. Monans boat *Beautiful Star,* whose memorial can be seen at Kings Lynn. His mother, being a Cellardyke woman, brought her young family back to Cellardyke, where Tam spent the remainder of his life as a Cellardyke fisherman. We stayed in his house when I was a primary school boy and, one year, a great shoal of cod set into the Traith after the winter herring fishing, feeding on herring spawn. My father, who had bought an 18 foot yawl from my mother's home town of Boddam, was persuaded by Tam and his two sons Adrian and Davie to launch the boat. There was no time to load proper ballast, so two bags filled with sand were put on board and we were away, to a sight of which I never saw an equal. Dozens of yawls of all description were surrounding a small area where the fish were. Men were shouting and yawls were even colliding with one another. There were fish galore, and even I was allowed to haul one up. On our return journey, with a stiffer breeze, Tam said, "gi'e the laddie a shot to steer" so, with father sitting at the sheet, and with me at the weather side of the tiller, we sped home. I have always been grateful to this rough man (who incidentally was one of the last men I saw chewing tobacco!) for insisting that I got my first turn at the helm. I was later to sail many of my father's visitor friends, with a westerly wind balanced against a flowing tide, and I could easily run for home if I saw anyone turning pale or ceasing to talk.

About 1930, father had a share in a 30 ft. motor yawl with 'Patchie' Watson, called the *Crest,* KY 35. She was a good sea boat and if they took visitors to the May Island I was allowed to go along. I was never allowed to go on the island by myself, but if there were others going ashore then I was able to accompany them and I enjoyed watching the seabirds, which developed into a lifelong hobby. Even today, May 18th 2000, I've been watching a baby blackbird in the garden, while listening to a lark and a chaffinch. The terns fascinated me and kittiwakes and terns remain my favourite sea birds to this day. Patchie and father had an agreement with Geordie Wilson, a fish merchant from Pittenweem, that if they had two boxes of codlins' or more, a phone call would bring him along.

He paid 12/6 (62°p) per box for a 7 stone box.

I didn't really like the sproules, with its associated vertical jerking. We were not as fly as the Pittenweem fishermen whom, I discovered much later, had developed a method whereby they could 'jerk' their lines with much less effort. By attaching the hoops normally used for holding the wooden staves of barrels in place to the outer rim of the gunwales, they were able to jerk their lines horizontally over the gunwales rather than vertically, the friction eventually wearing grooves in the wooden hoops. The result was that the 'Pittenweemers' caught the same amount of fish with much less effort.

Father and Patchie didn't keep the yawl very long as the engine gave too much trouble, so they sold it up north (at a good profit, of course!). Father then bought a 22ft. sailing yawl from Crail and Uncle Dave had a 7-9 Kelvin engine put in her, by Millers of St. Monans. He also had her decked with a rail on top of the old gunwales. It was in this yawl that I caught my biggest cod at the Sproules, at the 'meads' of 'Rankine's to the Coves'. There were trees at a farm which, long ago, was owned by a man named Rankine and, when these trees were seen in line with Caiplie Coves (between Crail and Cellardyke), you were at the right spot. As for our distance from the shore, we were certainly nearer to the May Island than the mainland, but I couldn't take you there today. I remember that cod although I was spewing my guts out at the time! Father noticed that it must be a big one, so he made his own line fast, grabbed the clip, and said to me "Easy now", while he whacked the gartlin hook, on the end of the clip, in to the back of the cod. "Now heave", he said, and between us we got it on board.

I mentioned I was sick. The first time I was sick was on a beautiful day, no wind, but the aftermath of a North Easterly storm. I was still a primary school boy and went away with father to the sproules in our first sailing yawl. We rowed towards the May as there was no wind. We caught the odd codlin, but the north-east swell was still there and I began to sweat, before being sick as never before or since. I became so bad that father decided we had better give up and he rowed us home himself, there still being no wind but this long, 'oily' swell. I was living at the time with my two aunts and uncle and, after struggling home, I said "Auntie, I'm no gaun again". I

21

called her Auntie, but she was really my father's Auntie Bawbie, born in 1854. "Just like your Grandfather", she said, "he was sick going along the street when he knew it was a north-easter".

Well, I sat on Auntie Annie's fender stool until she ushered me to bed, having felt as if I had been sailing all night. "You'll be all right after a sleep", she said, and she was right. Never again was I as bad, but I was nearly always sick with a north-easter although I grew accustomed to it. We often tried the sproules in the succeeding sail yawls after hauling the creels, but it was as much to get a fish for our tea as for sale. I must say I preferred the haurlins (hand lines), which had two hooks and a sinker (weight) attached instead of the sproule and baited with 'pelns', which mother's relatives from Boddam called 'peelers'. They were shore crabs about to cast their shell, which the alternate one was doing all summer from June onwards. To find 'pelns', you turned over the shore stones about half tide mark. After finding a crab, you broke off the hinged point of a big toe and, if the flesh that was disclosed was of a velvety appearance, that was a peln. They were stored in a small box, attached by string to the gunwale while in harbour to keep the crabs alive, until they were going to be used.

A trip to the 'haurlins' was pleasant of an evening, and your friends were always pleased to give you their company. While sitting anchored with a redd stone suspended over the side of the yawl, you took a peln out of the box, broke off the shell and tied it on to the hook with thread or wool. According to my father, he used to be sent up to the countryside to gather sheep's wool from the fences, which he called sheep's 'oo'. "Patience is a virtue at the haurlins", an old man once said to me, "but you're better wi' fresh pelns". Sometimes the man in the stern was catching steady while the man at the front was getting nothing. When his patience was exhausted he would say, "I'm going to haul up the redd stane and let her drift a wee bit, I'm obviously on the wrong side o' the skelly", and usually that evened things out.

The haurlins were always pleasant to go to as you only got pelns during the summer. They never cast their shells in cold weather.

One story about the haurlins. We were still staying in East Forth St., and my neighbour David Smith and I borrowed a dinghy from W. Band, gathered pelns and set out for a night's fishing. It didn't last long. We rowed south-east for about twenty minutes before throwing the redd stone over the side. We had hardly swung to the tide when we got bites. "I've got one," says David, "so have I," I said and for more than twenty minutes we were haulin' small codlins up two at a time. "I've got a bigger one this time" said David, so I made my line fast, looked over the side and said, "Wait". It was a good one and we didn't have a clip, so I said "I'll try to get a hand into it, while you haul". Well, we managed it, but I wondered later how we didn't capsize the 12 foot dinghy. Foolhardy! We lowered our lines again but, although they were still biting, the fish weren't swallowing the hook, so we never caught another that night. When we came into the harbour, Dr. Armour was on the pier and when we put our full box of codlins on the jetty where he kept his yawl, he said, "I've been to the May with George Mackay and we only got one fish".

When I asked my father why, after having caught so many fish, we were unable to catch any more as although the fish were still there they seemed to no longer like the bait, he replied that we had "just been there at the right time". No man can understand nature. As for the big fish that David caught, it spewed herring spawn out of its mouth.

After moving to West Anster David and I parted company, but I borrowed W. Bands' coble occasionally to go to the haurlins with my Wife (now of more than 50 years), Ann Page and her niece Sheila Fraser, now Mrs. Bill Blair. They were a good crew as they never got sick! I got a set of mackerel flies consisting of seventeen or eighteen hooks with feathers attached, and I cut them into three sets of six hooks as I got fed up clearing fouled line. We caught mackerel as we fished at about six or seven fathoms. On an afternoon when the sun was too high to catch mackerel, we discovered we could catch small codlins on these feathered hooks made fast to cat gut, so we didn't need to gather pelns. This passed a few summers, during which time Ann's niece, Sheila, changed from tomboy to young lady. Eventually I was left to go fishing alone, and I had had enough.

Before we leave the single hand manipulated fish line, I must mention the Jigs (or Jiggers as they were sometimes called in the Pittenweem Register, which existed from 1844-1855). I had a set of Jigs made for the museum by the late Harry Bowman. Jigs were made from metal knitting needles suspended horizontally and, from the end of each needle, were suspended hooks taken from a sma' line. Each jig was made from as many horizontal needles as you could manage (up to ten or twelve).

I never persuaded my father to try it, as it was mainly pursued at the May Island in July for herring. I have eaten the herring caught on the jigs, as an old man named Gay from Pittenweem used to sell them through the town. They tasted good and they were certainly better than Winter Herring, which were tasteless as their virtue had all gone into making roes.

My information now comes from Pittenweem fisherman Johnny Horsburgh and the late Jockie Gay, the latter being of Pittenweem who lived in Anster and whom I often consulted. Jockie Gay said that he went to the jigs in the summer months 'twelve fathoms to the Wast side of the May, one hour before dark and one hour before daylight'. The best shot he heard of was four crans of herring from five men. I asked him if they ever tried to catch them with nets and all he said was "they had too clear an eye to be caught with nets".

Well it's about time now to mention the sma' lines. There are many small creeks in our local area that would be acceptable places to haul up a coble or dinghy and could be a haven for a single person to pursue sma' line fishing from. I could see how it could be done from Boarhills, but I haven't heard of anyone fishing the sma' lines from that village. As for Kingsbarns, I have only heard of a family of Ritchies pursuing the creels from there. The Crailers, of course, were the top lobster fishers in our area and, as such, were naturally not keen to have this knowledge spread as to their success.

My father knew a lot of Crailers and so did I. They were great boys for nicknames, which I will not repeat at length. There were, however, one or two families of Smiths who were descended, as I was, not from the man who brought the whale's jaw bone to Cellardyke but from his father. There were three brothers whose nicknames were 'Wung', 'Towg' and 'Steamer'. I didn't know them personally but I certainly knew many of their descendants. Harry Smith, who died only recently, lived in the house down at the harbour, photographs of which have appeared on so many calendars. He owned the *Comely,* originally a Buckhaven boat, which he bought from Cellardyke. There is still a *Comely* today, but not the original one. Alfred Smith pursues the lobsters from Crail, but he is really a Dyker.

'Fifies' laid up on the Town's Green in Cellardyke

Harry Smith on the Crail creel boat *Comely*

An undated view of Cellardyke Harbour

One of the few stories I recall about the Crailers concerned 'Steamer', who was shooting a sma' line in a yawl with Eenie in thick fog. When the lines were all shot, Steamer remarked proudly, "Guessed her fine, Eenie, guessed her fine. That's 'Norman' (a big rock at the North Ness of the May Island) right ahead". Before they had time to rest for a while, however, the fog thinned out and the rock "right ahead" turned out to be the big rock down from Kilrenny Mill farm at the east end of Cellardyke, known as Basket Rock!

We'll move on now to Cellardyke as the Crailers were mainly creel lads. My father's sister, Auntie Annie (the one who saw that I did my lessons from the school), told me about gathering limpets down the seaside, but for most of the information about Cellardyke, we'll turn to Auld Wull (William Smith), who ended his working days as the Port Missionary at St. Andrews. He was my Father's cousin and I met him occasionally with my father when on a fraternal visit to see his brothers Tam and Jimmy, both fishermen.

Auld Wull wrote a series of biographical essays in the East Fife Observer in 1927, and I consider them of great value. "A fisherman usually married a woman belonging to his own place and own class", observed Wull, because a fisherman required a woman who could bait his lines as well as mend his nets. Cellardyke was a town of fishermen who lived somewhat primitively when William Smith was young, there being no running water in the houses and no wax cloth or linoleum on the floors. The wooden floors were washed with soap and water and sand was sprinkled over them. There was an interesting bit about the fishing boats in Auld Wull's essays, which said that "The main sail was usually bigger than the foresail". This arrangement must have changed before the advent of the camera, as I have never seen photographs of boats rigged in this manner. When at the line fishing, they carried eight of a crew, while four men tacked the foresail and four the mainsail. When engaged in herring fishing they only carried a foresail and sometimes a jib.

Auld Wull goes on to describe how the sma' line fishing lasted from the beginning of October to almost the turn of the year. The boats went to sea every day when the weather was favourable, going out on one tide and returning the next. The common thing was to bait six taes of line to a man, which amounted to forty-eight to a boat. The bait was chiefly mussels from Newhaven or Port Glasgow. Sometimes when mussels were scarce, limpets were used. Wull used to go up the country and gather grass by the side of the road or fields, which was spread out to wither at home. During the line fishing, the boats used Anster harbour more than Cellardyke. Cellardyke was used mainly when there was little wind and the sole means of propulsion was by the oars. When the boats went into Anster, it was the custom to put wet lines into a cart along with the 'kits', which were what each man kept his bread in. The youngest fisherman was sent along with the cart to show the carter where the members of the crew dwelt, so each man's lines and kit were put down at his door and on the cart's return the baited lines were taken to the boat. If a fisherman's lines were not baited when the cart came they had to be carried down to the boat afterwards.

If it was an early tide for the boats to go out, then they were back early and Wull remembered his mother rising at about four o'clock in the morning to get her lines baited in time. As he was the oldest of the family, Willliam Smith had to rise too and help her to shell the mussels. He recalled seeing her with a baby in the cradle and a string tied to her foot to rock the cradle whilst she used her hands to bait the lines. When the herring began to get scarce towards the end of March, the great line fishing commenced, the great lines being baited with herring. Then, when the herring were done, the haddock lines were baited and haddock was used as bait on the great lines. It was only the largest boats that went to the great lines.

Many of the boats, after the herring bait became scarce, did not always use all of their haddocks to bait the great lines, but sold them at the harbour if they had a good catch. At the winter lines, the haddocks were sold by the dozen, but in summer when they had bigger catches, they were sold by the hundred. They were divided into classes, big and small. In later years they came to be sold by the cwt., which was a better method, as previously the buyer and seller did not always agree about which fish were large and which were small. When his father was at sea and his mother was busy baiting lines, there was no time to make dinner, so Wull and his brothers got a 'piece' and were sent away to school. At tea time they got fish of some kind or other and used to enjoy fried flounders. There was always plenty of skull fish, which was the fish left on the line after the haddocks had been taken off. The curers only bought the haddocks, which they smoked in their kilns and sent them to Edinburgh and Glasgow markets. A great number of their skull fish were flounders, and they were sometimes so numerous that they were given away.

Wondering how to finish this chapter, I remembered Auld Wull saying that selling haddocks by classifying them as large or small was unpopular and they preferred to sell by weight. In writing the *Lammas Drave* (John Donald, Edinburgh, 1985), I was fortunate enough to borrow from Robbie Gardner the diary which belonged to his Great-Granda (Venus Peter). In there I found an example of each:

1866, December 29th - 150 dozen large at 1/3d. Small 3/- Cod 4/3   £9. 4. 3d.

1869 January 7th - 1 ton 2 cwt. 3 qtrs. 0 lbs. £15. 13/- (VenusPeter's first winter line trip).

Carmi winter line fishing 1868 January 9th: 1 ton 6 cwt. 1qtr.7 lbs. cost 31- £13.14.6d.

A wintry view of Crail harbour, with the storm booms in place at the harbour mouth

Anstruther Harbour in 1873

Boats in the old West Harbour at Pittenweem

Anster, Cellardyke and Pittenweem, up to 1918

From the first Statistical Account 1791-99 for the Parish of Pittenweem by the Rev. Jas. Nairn:

"The fish caught here of late have been of a much smaller number than formerly. Quantities are sometimes sent to the Edinburgh market. A considerable quantity of lobsters are caught here and in the neighbourhood and sent to London. At present only five boats and four vessels, although prior to 1639 the shipping here was considerable. From then to 1645 the town suffered greatly. Then there belonged thirteen sail of large vessels, all of which were taken by the enemy after the battle of Kilsyth. The population at present is 1157. This was increased by Sir John Anstruther's coal and salt works".

The *Second Statistical Survey* was by the Rev. John Cooper in 1845, who gave the population for 1831 as 1,317 and for 1847 as 1,379. Rev. Cooper stated that there was a considerable number of fishing boats in the district, but as Anster Easter had the better harbour the fishing was chiefly connected with that port, which had "a few sloops and schooners", but no actual numbers were given. According to the book *History of Fife up to 1840* by John M. Leighton, Pittenweem is one of the creeks of Anster Easter and their fishing fleet statistics are included therein.

On looking at Anster Easter, the survey reported that two packets sail weekly to and from Leith. Six persons are engaged in fish curing and the number of barrels marked at Anster, including its creeks, was 40,000, selling at 22/- per barrel, which amounted to £44,000. In 1838 there were one hundred boats, each having a crew of five men and an average take of four hundred barrels.

Before I refer to the *Pittenweem Register,* I will quote from some notes I took from the late Jocky Gay, a Pittenweem man who was married to an Anster woman and lived his married life in Anster.

"A line in Pittenweem has 5 taes, each hook three and a half feet apart from its neighbour. There are one hundred and twenty hooks on a taes, so a line had six hundred hooks and was more than seventy fathoms long. In Pittenweem the snade was made of the same hemp material as the line, while the part called the hemp in Pittenweem was actually twisted horse's hair.

When redding the line the hook was twisted into the hemp and the line was thus easier tidied up.

The hooks used in Pittenweem were numbers 19 and 20. The Pittenweem hemp, was 5 or 6 horse hairs twisted together. In Cockenzie the snade was thinner and longer. In Pittenweem, the lines weighed 1lb. 4oz. to the taes. The crew was usually of five men, each with two lines of six hundred hooks. Bait was often a problem; the Tayport mussels were softer than the Eden mussels. They sometimes had to send to Wales and King's Lynn for mussels. They even baited with herring. The herring arrived from Eyemouth with the 4 p.m. train, and one herring provided thirty two baits. Since the baiting only started after all the baits had been cut the lines were not shot until 10 p.m."

He also gave me some information about the 'Jigs'. The best area to use Jigs was twelve fathoms to the west of the May Island, one hour before dark and one hour before daylight. The best shot he heard of was four cran of herring for five men at the Jigs. On my enquiring why they didn't try to catch them with winter herring nets, the answer I got was "Too clear an eye to be caught with nets."

A Chronology of the Inshore Fishing Industry in Anster, Cellardyke and Pittenweem from 1844 to 1918.

The information has been taken mainly from the *Pittenweem Register* and the *East Fife Record*, with the dates quoted referring to the edition of the newspaper in question:

1844

May 3: Haddock fishing very successful this week, but prices do not compensate for the labours of the fishermen.

Aug. 8: One man caught sixteen dozen at the Jiggers.

1852

Oct. 28: Great storm. Crail pier damaged. Three fishing boats dashed to pieces on the Craignoon rock. Ninety yards of new bulwark at Cellardyke damaged. In East Anster large stones were carried up as far as the Town Hall by the sea.

1855

Dec. 2: Mr. Scott, Editor of the *Pittenweem Register*, died on the 9th. A great deal of news about a cholera epidemic.

1857

The *East Fife Record* first produced. Information taken from the newspaper that year indicates that the local fishing fleet, consisting of 30 partially decked boats, caught two hundred and fifty score of white fish (chiefly haddock) fishing seventy miles out to sea. Each vessel had a crew of eight men, each having 15 taes of one hundred and twenty hooks.

1862

June 7: One curer purchased 1,700 dozen white fish which were smoked for the Glasgow market. The spring was cold and wet. Twenty five yawls engaged at the creels.

1863

<u>May 16</u>: Some boats reported catches of 250-350 dozen haddocks at sixpence per dozen.

<u>May 30</u>: Jigs at May Island as high as a cran. Three shillings and eight pence per dozen.

1865

<u>April 28:</u> Some boats landed 100 dozen very small haddocks, selling at 7/- per hundred.

<u>Aug. 18</u>: Great number of cod landed.

1866

<u>Feb. 2</u>: Many large cod caught from hand lines, selling at 1/6 to 2/6 each.

<u>March 9</u>: Great haddock fishing.

1868

Haddock fishing closed. A poor year.

<u>Jan. 3</u>: No telegraph between here and Thornton for gale warnings.

1869

<u>Jan. 15</u>: End of good haddock fishing.

<u>Sept. 3</u>: Good shots of cod between the May Island and the shore.

1872

<u>Jan 12</u>: Good haddock fishing.

1873

<u>Jan 17</u>: 320 tons haddock landed during the season, compared with 300 tons the previous year. 1 ton of haddock was approximately equal to 23 boxes.

1874

<u>Jan 30</u>: 5 tons haddock landed, selling at 17/6 per cwt. Pittenweem reporting success at the haddock fishing. The St. Monans fishermen were

pursuing the trawl - unprecedented at this time of year.
Feb. 6: 9 tons of haddock landed.

1875
Jan. 15: Good haddock and cod fishing. No ling or halibut landed. 55 tons of haddock landed.
Jan. 22: 84 tons of haddocks landed, selling at 15/- per cwt.
Feb. 5: 20 tons of haddocks landed.
Feb. 19: Large number of cod caught on hand lines.

1876
Jan. 14   40 tons haddocks landed.
Jan. 21   37 tons haddocks landed.
Mar. 2   Cod plentiful.

1877
Jan. 5: 38 tons of haddocks cured by Tom Brown.
Jan. 19: 120 tons of haddocks landed during the week, worth £1,300.
June 8: Death of Capt. Rodger.
Aug. 3: Beam trawling was forbidden in the 'Traith' in 1862. As this ban had caused no improvement in fish stocks, it was allowed again.

1878
Jan. 11: 54 boats landed 29 tons of haddocks.

1879
Jan 26: Worst snow for 40 years. 61 boats reported catches of between 5 and 21° cwt. Total fish landed 22 tons at 12/6 per cwt.
Feb. 7: Few ling caught, but cod plentiful, selling at between 9d to 1/- each. Pittenweem fisherman D.Parker had the top catch of 48° cwt. of haddock.
Feb. 28: Haddock scarce, selling at 11/- to 13/6 per cwt.
April 4: Cod fishing so poor that boats took the unusual step to revert to the 'sma' lines'. Nineteen boats, each fishing with 7 lines, landed 6 tons of haddock.

April 25: More fish than at any time this year.

1885
March 6: Pittenweem fishermen complaining about steam trawlers.
June 26: Pittenweem - 1 box of jig herring caught at the May Island fetched 12/-.
July 10: Good prices for Pittenweem jig herring caught at the May and in the Traith.

1887
Jan 14: It was claimed that the new electric light on the May could be seen 46 miles out to sea.
Feb. 4: Due to abolition of the ban on beam trawling, 100 boxes of plaice were caught in St. Andrews bay.
Apr. 29: Wheel used for steering instead of the 'tully' for the first time.
July 1: 6 yawls at the 'jigs' caught 300 - 400 herring, which sold at 3/- to 4/- per 100.

1888
Feb. 10: Foundation of Anster Rangers Football Club.
June 1: The book *Anster* is published by G. Gourlay.
Sept. 14: It was claimed that the May light could be seen 61 miles out to sea.

1889
Mar. 15: Fish prices (per stone) - Cod 1/3 to 1/6, Ling 2/6 to 3/6, Skate 2/6 to 3/6 and Halibut 6/-.
June 21: Yawls reported to be catching 100 to 200 herring each at jigs, selling at 5/- per hundred.
June 28: During the previous 6 months, cod landings at Anster realised £13,000, with Herring fetching £10,000.

1890
Feb. 7: Large haddocks caught between St. Abb's head and Berwick. Line

Pittenweem fisherman Lock Horsburgh redding a line

Sma' lines being baited by W.Wood and M.Wilson at Pittenweem during the 1930's
(Cowie Collection)

Launch of the 'Bauldie' *Orion* KY183 at Anster in 1927 for A.Doig of Cellardyke. She was a boat I was often aboard as my father was one of her first crew members.

The *Ocean Venture* KY209, owned by Tom Gardner, pictured at the end of the East Pier in Anster.

boats landed 30-40 boxes each.

April 18: Cellardyke boat *Garland* lost with all hands.

April 25: Serious depression in the fishing industry. Value of fish landings for the three previous years in the district were £21,000 for 1887-1888; £15,000 for 1888-1889 and £5,200 for 1889 - 1890.

Actual quantity of fish landed:

	Cod (cwt.)	Haddock (cwt.)	Crabs (Hundreds)
1888	2974	2502	3615
1889	2108	1400	2678

Dec. 5: Steam liners doing well.

1891

Jan. 30: Demand for afternoon fish train from Anster as well as forenoon.

Feb 20: Most of the boats were going to the lines as herring prices very poor.

1892

Jan 12: Cod selling at 35/- per score.

1897

Feb. 19: Pittenweem haddock selling at 2/- to 5/- per box.

April 9: Haddock yawls landing at Pittenweem and St. Monans: Haddocks fetching 7/- to 9/- per box. Catches ranging from 1˘ - 5 boxes per boat (presumably 7 stone boxes).

April 25: Pittenweem boats catching as many as 5 boxes of haddock fishing outside the May Island. Prices 12/3 to 12/9 per box.

May 14: Pittenweem reports good catches of cod from 'ripper'.

May 28: Pittenweem reports mixed fishing. Some boats employed at the 'jig' herring and some fishing the sma' lines using sand eels for bait.

July 2: Most of the Pittenweem yawls at the sma' lines. Catches averaging 1 - 3 boxes.

July 23: Pittenweem boats reverted to mussel bait.

<u>Aug. 13</u>: 40 boats fishing from Anster, chiefly Newhaven yawls.

1898
<u>May 27</u>: Pittenweem boats employed at the 'jig' herring.

1899
Value of all kinds of fish for June:

	1899	1898
Anstruther District	£3,289	£1,690
Pittenweem	319	540
St. Monans	810	689
Crail and Kingsbarns	119	287
Totals:	£5,513	£4,227

<u>April 28</u>: Haddock yawls report few catches.
<u>May 5</u>: The total amount of boats in the district propelled by oars or sails is 544, with an overall weight of 7682 tons. The quantity of fish carried by rail over the last year was 2,489 tons from Anster station, 243 tons from Pittenweem and 233 from Crail.

1900
<u>Jan 12</u>: Cod fetching £3.10/- to £5 per score, ling 2/- to 3/- each and skate 3/- each.
<u>Feb. 9</u>: Fulton built a bauldie for Fisherrow, with more orders expected.
<u>Sept. 28</u>: 20 years lease of Victoria Hotel from Mr. Dunsire to Post Office

1901
<u>Feb. 15</u>: School report states that there are currently 535 pupils at Cellardyke school.
<u>Feb. 22</u>: BaillieWilliamson bought the old infant school in Cellardyke for conversion to houses.

1903

May 1: Fulton launched M.B. *Hughes*.

1904

Jan. 1: Cellardyke harbour fit for use again following the rebuilding of the east pier. The pier had been washed down during the great storm of 1898.

Feb. 9: Fishery Cruiser *Brenda* is seen off Anster for first time in many months, no trawlers seen on Sunday.

Feb. 12: School roll at Cellardyke reported to be 584, with 94 attending Kilrenny School.

May 12: East Neuk Fishing Fleet Statistics:

Anster had 11 steam drifters. Anster and Cellardyke: 142 boats, 434 resident and 163 non resident fishermen; Pittenweem: 66 boats, 227 resident, 92 non resident fishermen; St. Monans: 100 boats 372 resident, 20 non-resident fishermen; Crail and Kingsbarns: 42 boats and 73 men.

Oct. 9: : Fishery Cruiser *Brenda* caught trawler *Albatross* of Leith poaching for the 12th time. Fines ranged from £20-£50.

1905

June 14: New crane installed at Pittenweem harbour to enable heavier storm booms to be lifted into place.

1906

Jan. 26: Pittenweem boats reported to be at the sma' lines. The total amount of boats and bauldies fishing from St. Monans is 59.

1908

April 17: Cod selling at £2. 6/- per score. Halibut priced at 8/6 each.

1909

Jan 14: Leading lights installed at the head of the East Pier at Anster.

1910

Feb. 17: Pittenweem Skipper Andrew Anderson ordered a Gardner engine for his boat, which will be fitted at Cockenzie.

Mar. 3: Fulton of Pittenweem has completed a 30ft motor yawl for the line fishing. The vessel is fitted with a 7HP 2 cylinder Kerosene engine and has been built for J. S. Paterson, merchant, the Shore.

Mar. 31: New motor yawl built at Pittenweem for James Hughes (Wood) for sma' line fishing.

April 7: New gym opened at Waid Academy, with retiring rooms and lavatories. Sergeant Vine appointed janitor. Live herrings found in cods' mouths at the sproules.

April 14: New yawl launched at Pittenweem by Fulton. Christened *Grei,* she is 30ft long and fitted with an engine.

May 5: Trial trip of *Grei*. Miller launched a yawl measuring 27ft by 10ft, bound for Arbroath.

May 26: Andrew Anderson's new motor boat *Majestic* arrived at Pittenweem last week. Dimensions 73ft x 20ft and fitted with a 95HP engine.

Nov. 3: M.B. *Majestic* lands 23 crans at Yarmouth

1911

Feb. 9: Bauldies reported to be fishing better than boats.

April 13: The fishing port of Eyemouth now has 35 motor boats.

April 27: Youths charged for playing football in the street with a cork.

July 2: Water cut off in Cellardyke from 3 p.m. to 9 a.m. The old well at Urquhart Wynd was re-opened to provide supplies.

Nov. 2: Miller to build 28ft Anster yawl for J. Davidson, St. Monans.

Dec. 14: Proposals to convert the field at Bankie Park into a recreation ground.

1912

Jan.4: Value of fish landings for 1910 and 1911 published:

	1911	1910
Anster	£14,700	£17,400
Pittenweem	3,040	4,900
St. Monans	5,100	5,100
Crail and Kingsbarns	2,900	3,100
Totals:	£25,740	£30,500

Feb 1: *Daily Mail* says Anster has a population of 4,300.
June 2: *Quiet Waters* to be fitted with a 7HP Grei engine.
Sept. 5: St. Monans best fished of local fleets at the drave.

1914

Jan. 11: Fishing statistics published:

	1912	1913
Sail Boats	421	373
Creels	4,290	4,340
Motor Boats	10	27
Steam Drifters	60	64
Fishermen (local)	1,385	1,386
Non-resident	552	368
Coopers	-	104

June 14: Fishermen not under Insurance Act listed as 'Joint Adventurers'.
Sept. 14: Inshore line fishermen to send cargoes to Glasgow.
Dec. 3: Unrestricted fishing in St. Andrews bay. At Pittenweem, 23 local yawls were prohibited from line fishing.

1915

Jan 21: Line fishing is allowed within half a mile of the low water mark, from vessels under 30ft.
Crail fishermen report good line fishing, but the anchor nets have been a

failure.

Jan. 28: Sudden death of A. Thomson, boat builder.

May 6: Yawl *Sunbeam,* measuring 29˚ft by 10ft 8inches and fitted with a 15HP engine, launched at St Monans for R. Cargill, Arbroath.

Aug. 19: Report that the fleet of motor yawls has doubled in a year.

Landings from the sma' lines in 1915 compared with 1913:

	Number of Boats	Weight of Fish Landed (cwt.)	Value of Fish Landed
1915	39	480	£29,991
1913	26	320	£10,969

1916

Sept. 7: British Summer Time, which had been implemented in May, was regarded as a great success. It was scheduled to end on 1 October.

Dec. 28: One basket of codlings landed at Crail.

1917

30 yawls at St. Monans reported to be fishing within one mile of the shore, which should help the line fishing.

Feb. 22: Cod net fishing proved very successful, with catches of 7-11 score per boat reported. The fish was mainly sold at Pittenweem for between 5/- and 8/6 each for prime cod. Fulton launched a 40ft bauldie at Pittenweem with a 30HP Kelvin engine for Jas. Wood of St. Monans, named *Julia Wood*.

April 5: Cod prices ranging from 6/- to 8/6 each.

April 26: Closure of West Anster Post Office after 18 years.

Oct. 4: 6 St. Monans motor boats and 1 Anster boat left for the south accompanied by the usual convoy.

1918

April 4: Cod fetching 11/3 per stone. Obituary to the late Capt. John Keay

Oct. 24: 'Flu epidemic in east Fife.

Nov. 7: All schools closed due to 'flu epidemic.

Nov. 14: News of peace reached Anster after midday on Monday. Cellardyke Town Hall bell rope broke as it was pulled to celebrate peace and was never mended (the bell was shown to me by Jim Williamson, who was pulling it with Robbie Wallace at the time).

Nov. 28: Last Thursday forenoon, in bright sunshine, double lines of British warships with the German Fleet between them sailed up the Forth all day. Some anchored in Largo Bay, others near Inchkeith.

The crew of the *Winaway* KY279. They are (left to right) Robert Smith, Jock Brown, Sandy Parker, John Smith, David Gourlay and John Gourlay.

In Pittenweem West Harbour

Robina (left) and Margaret Horsburgh shelling mussels at Pittenweem

Pittenweem from 1919 - a Chronology

The following extracts concerning the Pittenweem fishing industry and other local events have been taken from the local press. Again, the dates refer to the edition of the newspaper from which the information has been extracted:

1919

Feb. 7: Highest catch 50 stones at a controlled price. Good supplies of white fish.

Feb. 14: White fish poor compared with previous week.

Mar. 7: Cod net fishing only half as good as the previous year.

June 19: Pittenweem residents get an excellent view of Britain's biggest airship, as it passed over on a trial flight before departing for America.

July 26: Peace day celebrations last Saturday. A beacon was lit on Kellie Law and others could be seen on Berwick Law and Arthur's seat.

July 31: Anster & Cellardyke fishermen on strike but not the Pittenweem and St. Monans men.

Aug. 28: Line fishing moderate success, best catch 3 boxes of large haddocks.

Sept. 18: Fishermen's strike ended after 9 weeks.

Dec. 4: Fulton's yard sold to D. & A. Reekie.

1920

Jan 13: 1 bauldie landed 91/4 cwt. of fish at controlled price from the cod nets.

Feb. 26: District saw 250 cwt. of white fish landed with a value of £380.

Mar. 27: Line fishermen are having a good time. Many fishermen over 70 have gone back to sea after being retired.

April 3: Cod as high as 15/- per stone and line at 8/- per stone.

1923

Jan 18: Pittenweem auction to be held each week day at about 11 a.m. as the boats were now arriving back in port around 10 am.

Mar. 29: A. Wood of *Rockvilla* caught a seal in cod nets measuring 4'2" by 2'9".

Aug. 16: White fish scarce so price high.

Nov. 8: Haddocks so scarce they were fetching 40/- per box. Codlings more plentiful at 20/- to 30/- per box.

Dec. 27: Line fishing improved with catches as high as 6 boxes. Monday market prices: haddock 65/- per box, codlings 35/- per box. Tuesday market prices: haddock 41/- to 47/- per box., codlings 25/- to 27/- per box.

1925

Sept. 3: Pittenweem line fishing has had a good year.

1926

Feb. 18: Weather having been so bad, the booms were only taken off the harbour mouth this week.

Mar. 11: Most of the fleet at the cod fishing. T. Black of Pittenweem landed 60-70 score of cod.

1927

Jan. 13: Some Pittenweem and St. Monans bauldies reported to be fishing at Rothesay.

Aug. 18: Daily catches averaging 1 box of haddocks per boat.

Dec. 29: Pittenweem boats fishing well at Rothesay.

1928

Pittenweem yawls again fishing at Rothesay.

1929

Oct. 24: Pittenweem fishing season at Rothesay has not been good. Local boats have returned to Pittenweem to go to the lines.

1930

Nov. 27: Pittenweem booms on for past week due to weather.

Dec. 11: *Golden Chance* launched by Aitken for J. Bowman. Fitted with 30 HP Kelvin engine.

1931

Jan. 8: *Boy Alex* launched by Aitken for J. Wood. Dimensions 34ft by 12ft and fitted with a 30 HP Kelvin engine.

Jan. 12: *Eulogia* launched by W. Reekie for Miss H. Landing, Pittenweem. Length 25ft. with 30 HP Kelvin. Local boats still fishing at Rothesay.

Mar. 12: Storm booms in place at Pittenweem.

Apr. 16: Cod net fishing now closed and haddock lines started.

Apr. 23: Herring shoals reported off Pittenweem accompanied by a large number of cod. Pittenweem fishermen voice their disapproval of the seine net, which they say will destroy the haddock line fishing.

Apr. 30: St. Monans men accuse Pittenweem men of doing damage to herring spawn with cod nets. Pittenweem contends that during the 15 years the nets have been in use, the herring have been plentiful. More poaching in the Firth by Cockenzie and Port Seton seine net fishermen.

June 18: T. Johnston 79, sail maker, died in Pittenweem.

Aug. 20: In this period of depression, Pittenweem fish curers were still successful.

Nov. 26: J. Masson of Pittenweem to join the Life Guards.

Dec. 31: *Enterprise*, 36 ft. long and fitted with a 30HP Kelvin engine, built for Aitken and McKay of Pittenweem by W. Reekie.

1932

Jan. 7: Pittenweem motor boats left Rothesay for home.

Mar. 3: School rolls: Waid Academy 343, Cellardyke 386, St. Monans 211, Pittenweem 188, Crail 199 & Elie 97.

Mar. 17: Good landings of cod reported at Pittenweem.

Mar. 24: Pittenweem cod net yawls strike heavy shoals feeding on herring spawn. Catches exceeded 20 score, for which there was little demand, so some of the yawls landed at Newhaven.

April 7: Granary bought by Bowman, fish salesman.

May 5: Pittenweem line fishing has poor results.

1934

Feb. 15: *Aurora* of Pittenweem sunk off Crail. Crew rescued by *Comely*.

Mar. 24: Pittenweem cod fetching 2/- to 2/6 per stone.

Aug. 2: Deaths reported of Capt. David Burd of Pittenweem and Capt. Laverock of Crail.

Aug. 30: No assistance for bauldies under Government scheme.

Oct. 4: Death of Sir Ralph Anstruther.

1935

Jan. 17: Good supplies of cod from cod nets on Monday, selling at 4/- per stone. Favourable landings reported by line boats.

Jan. 24: Codlings fetching 14/6 - 18/9 per box at Pittenweem. Haddocks scarce, prices 33/- to 36/- per box. New Herring Bill praised by Henderson Stewart M.P. when he addressed the Auchtermuchty Women Liberals.

Jan. 31: Pittenweem codling prices: 1 -5 boxes fetching 22/- to 24/6 per box. Light catches of codlings, 1 - 4 boxes: 17/6 to 19/9 per box.

Feb. 14: All the local boats were now pursuing the cod net and herring fishing. On Monday, 60 score of cod landed which sold at 2/6 to 3/- per stone. Best shot reported to be 10 score. Tuesday landings consisted of Cod and spraggs, with the best shot 6 score. Prices 2/9 to 3/3 per score.

Feb. 21: Monday landings from cod nets: 40 score of cod, best shot 10 score. Prices 3/- to 3/3 per score. Cod was scarce on Tuesday, selling at 2/6 per stone.

Feb. 28: Boats in port on Monday due to storm. Tuesday landings: 70 score cod selling at 3/- to 3/6 per stone.

Mar. 7: Pittenweem reports good landings during the past week. Monday: 100 score cod at 3/- per stone; Tuesday 40 score cod at 3/- to 3/6 per stone.

Mar .14: Monday stormy. On Tuesday, 18 boats landed 110 score cod at 1/6 - 2/- per stone.

Mar. 21: Monday 80 score cod 1/6 to 1/9 per stone. 15 boxes codlings 7/6 to 10/- per box; Tuesday 30 score cod at 2/3 per stone; Wednesday 30 score cod at 2/6 to 3/- per stone.

Mar. 28: Monday very light supplies of cod. Prices 9d to 2/6 each; Tuesday codling 13/- per box.

April 4: Monday 35 score cod at 2/9 per stone, Spraggs 2/6 per stone. 30 boxes codlings landed, selling at 10/- to 11/9 per box. Catfish 1/- each; Tuesday 10 score cod at 3/- to 3/3 per stone.

April 11: Poor landings last week. Monday: cod selling at 4/6 - 5/- per stone; Tuesday 25 score cod landed seling at 5/- per stone.

April 18: Most boats stopped winter herring. Monday: 100 score cod landed, selling at 3/6 - 4/- per stone with 80 score cod fetching 5/- per stone.

May 9: Jubilee Celebrations. On Monday, 10 boats landed good catches at Pittenweem: 45 boxes of codlings at 12/6 to 16/- per box, Sole 1/6d, catfish 7d. Haddocks: small shots fetching 8/- per stone. Tuesday: 40 boxes codlings 11/- to 13/9 per box.

May 16: All line boats at sea. Majestic 1 - 4 boxes. Monday - 50 boxes codlings at 12/6 to 16/- per box; Tuesday: 10 boats, 30 boxes 12/- to 16/- per box. Small landings of haddocks.

May 23: All line boats at sea. Monday: 20 boxes of codlings at 20/6 to 23/6 per box; Tuesday: 10 boats, 27 boxes of codlings, 20/6 to 22/6 per box.

July 4: Five of the local boats leave for Dundee next week to carry fuel for the sea planes operating at Newport.

Aug. 27: Steam trawler *Gareloch* ashore at Billowness.

Sept. 19: Motor boat *Hughes* burnt off Billowness on way from Pittenweem to Anster.

1936

Jan 2: Monday: all line boats at sea. Shots of 1 -4 boxes of codlings; Tuesday: 5 boats, 1- 3 boxes selling at 15/6 per box.

Jan. 9: Pittenweem boats at cod nets. Monday: 7 boats landed 40 score at 5/- per stone.

Jan. 16: Aitken launched a super Bauldie, *Emulate*, for T. Aitken, St. Monans and J. Hughes, Pittenweem. Measuring 56ft by 17ft, she was fitted with a 8HP Rinton Horneby diesel engine. The engine room was situated at the fore side of the cabin and galley, behind the wheel house.

Jan. 23: Death of King George V on 14th.

Feb. 6: All cod net boats at sea. Cod fetching 4/- per stone.

Feb. 20: Monday: cod net boats land 75 score cod with the best shot 12 score. Price 4/- per stone.

Feb. 27: Pittenweem cod selling at 4/- to 5/- per stone.

Mar. 5: Monday: 12 cod net boats landed 30 score cod, selling at 3/- to 3/6 per stone. Tuesday: 30 score cod landed.

Mar. 12: Monday: 100 score cod landed, fetching 3/- to 4/- per stone; Tuesday: 4 cod net boats fishing, best shot 14 score.

Mar. 19: Monday: 56 score cod landed, prices 2/- to 2/6 per stone; Tuesday: 136 score cod landed.

Mar. 26: *Courageous II* launched by W. Reekie for the Wilson family. Dimensions 46ft by 15ft. On Monday, 8 cod net boats landed 26 score cod at 2/6 per stone; Tuesday: 11 score cod at 3/6 per stone. Andrew Boyter of Cellardyke (my Father's uncle), former skipper of *Bonita* and *Storm King*, died in Pittenweem aged 92. He also assisted his son-in-law in the *Tulip*.

Apr. 9: Monday: all cod net boats out. 130 score cod and spraggs landed, selling at 3/6 - 4/6 per stone; Tuesday: 145 score cod landed.

Apr. 16: 31 score cod landed at Pittenweem, fetching 3/- to 3/6 per stone. A start has been made to line fishing.

Apr. 30: Monday: 78 score cod selling at 3/- to 3/6 per stone.

May 28: *Argosy* launched by Reekie for Alan Lawson. Length 53ft and fitted with an 80HP National engine.

Sept 17: 13 Pittenweem boats employed at line fishing.

Sept. 26: *Floral Queen* launched at Anster by Reekie. Dimensions 47ft by 15ft 6in and fitted with a 63 HP engine.

1937

Jan. 21: Pittenweem port closed with booms in place due to weather.

Feb. 4: *Margaret Lawson* ashore in fog at Billowness bathing pool.

Feb. 11: *Margaret Lawson* breaks up and only the engine is saved. 12 Cod net boats land 2 to 10 score cod at 3/6 - 4/- per stone.

Feb. 18: Monday: 12 boats land shots of 1 - 8 boxes, prices 3/6 - 4/- per stone.

Feb. 25: Report states that in 1936 the booms at the harbour entrance were in use on 34 days. (Booms were first used after alterations to the harbour in

J.Wood (far right) baiting sma' lines at Pittenweem during the 1930's (Cowie Collection)

Line boats entering Pittenweem Harbour. The booms which were put in place during stormy weather can be seen lying on the pier. I've been told there were fourteen booms.

Fish laid out for sale at the West Pier, Pittenweem, c.1939 (Cowie Collection)

Local boats *Volunteer*, *Launch Out* and *Courageous II* in the Inner Harbour at Pittenweem, along with the Newhaven boat *Robina Wilson* (LH165)

1903). The number of fishermen currently working from Pittenweem stands at between 250 and 300.

Mar. 4: Monday: 12 cod net boats landed 70 score cod.

Mar. 11: Monday: 11 boats landed 60 score cod, with the best shot 17 score. Prices 2/6 to 3/- per stone.

Mar. 18: Monday: 18 cod net boats landed 50 score cod, selling at 1/- to 1/6 per stone.

Mar. 25: Monday: 12 cod net boats landed 150 score cod and spraggs, prices 2/6 - 3/6 per stone; Tuesday: 55 score cod and spraggs landed.

May 13: Coronation of King George VI celebrated yesterday.

June 24: Anniversary of Isle of May disaster.

Sept 30: Monday: 13 line boats landed 1-3 boxes of cod and spraggs at 5/- to 9/- per stone. Dabs selling at 5/- to 6/- per stone; codlings 20/6 to 21/6, large haddocks 27/6, medium 30/6 to 31/6, small 30/- to 32/- (all per box); lemon soles 8d to 1/8d, catfish 1/- to 1/9 each. There were improved supplies on Tuesday.

Nov. 25: Monday: 16 boats landed 1 to 8 boxes, cod and spraggs fetching 2/6 to 3/- per stone.

1938

Jan. 6: Good catches of white fish by local boats, prices up to £3.12/-. 12 boats landed between 1 to 12 boxes. Cod and spraggs selling at 2/- to 2/6 per stone.

Jan. 13: Monday: 12 cod net boats landed 25 score cod with the best shot 4 score. Cod and spraggs fetching 30/per score. Saithe 1/- each; Tuesday: 10 cod net boats and 5 line boats landed between 1 to 4 boxes.

Jan. 20: Improved landings. Monday: Catches averaging 5 - 10 boxes, selling at 4/6 to 5/- per stone; Tuesday: 5 boats landed 7 boxes at 11/6 to 16/- per box.

Jan. 27: A superb display of the Aurora Borealis was witnessed in the area. Some local residents claimed they had never seen it better. Saturday: 1 boat landed 2 boxes at 10/- per box. Wednesday: 2 boxes landed, prices 14/3 to 14/9 per box.

Feb. 3: Wednesday: 6 boxes landed at 10/6 per box.

Sept. 8: A house was hit by lightning in Pittenweem, rendering the family occupying the property deaf for hours.

Oct. 6: Lachlan McInnes retired as lighthouse keeper on the May Island

1939

Feb. 2: Pittenweem boats at haddock lines.

March 16: 16 boats engaged at line fishing.

April 30: Local man W. Birrell is appointed Manager of Chelsea F.C.

July 20: 17 boats employed at lines.

Nov. 30: Death of James Hughes of *Olive* (the *Olive* was the boat nearest to the *Mohawk* when she was bombed).

1940

Jan. 4: Decision taken not to disclose the values of fish landed during each month.

Feb. 21: Booms in place at Pittenweem harbour entrance all week.

Apr. 18: Report in the *Daily Record* states that the average wage of local fishermen is £70 to £80 per week. Skippers reported to be earning as much as £500.

1941

Jan. 23: Stirrup pumps can be purchased for £1.

May 1: Higher prices for fish. On Tuesday, the price for one halibut was £7. 12/- . On Wednesday the price was £6. 6/-.or 1 halibut. On Saturday, the price for one turbot was £1. 2/6. Pittenweem was bombed with two bombs which did not explode. The bombs landed near the bus station on the south side of Toll Cross. Nobody injured.

May 8: Price of fish to be controlled by June 1. Double summer time was announced on May 15.

Sept. 11: Line fishermen complaining that the price for un-gutted fish had been reduced from 7/2 ha'penny to 6/1 ha'penny per stone. The price for the same fish in October 1938 had been 7/- per stone, but costs had increased 3 fold since then.

<u>Nov. 6</u>: Death of local resident John Heinenen, a native of Finland. It was announced that Rev. Dinwoodie was to take up the position of Minister at Pittenweem.

1945

<u>May 10</u>: V.E. (Victory in Europe) celebrated.

<u>July 19</u>: Announcement that echo sounders are to be fitted to fishing boats.

<u>July 24</u>: Retiral of Dr. Wilson.

<u>Aug. 9</u>: Death of Harrison Cooper, the music teacher.

<u>Aug. 16</u>: Surrender of Japan.

<u>Dec. 20</u>: Shore fishermen are to be included in the Insurance Bill.

1951

It becomes more evident that the seine net is dominating the local fishing industry, therefore it seems fitting to close with:

<u>Feb. 8</u>: *Hope* and *Good Design* reverted to line fishing.

About 25-30 years ago I was taking an evening stroll to the Billowness. On going down Bankwell Road, I spoke to Mrs. Jockie Gay in her garden.
"That was a good shot they had yesterday." I said.
"Yes" she said "40 boxes, but nothing the day. Jockie said that the sile (sand eels) had all shifted east on to the hard ground and the codlins had followed them".
Well, I knew that meant that the fish had moved to the east of the rock known as 'Johnnie Doo's Pulpit', where it was hard ground.

Many years later I was pursuing the same route and, about the middle of the Hynd, met an elderly Pittenweem man. We stopped to talk and I said, "What are these two boats doing? That's hard ground there!" Their manoeuvres were in this identical area where Jockie Gay's crew were unable to go with their ordinary seine net.
"That's pair trawling" he said. I enquired about their catch the next day, and I was told they had caught "nothing but small codlins". I've been informed since that it was this same 'pair trawling' that ruined the inshore

fisheries.

And so it has gone on, with the 'pair trawling' men blaming the 'prawn fishers' and vice versa for there being no white fish close to the shore any more. It's something that maybe can't be proved, but if it is true then there should be a limit imposed similar to the old 'three mile limit'.

The *Launch Out* (ML455) and *Ivy Leaf* (ML166) in Pittenweem Harbour

Pittenweem fisherman John Horsburgh redding a line

KY 641 *Express* and ML39 *Sparkling Waters* in St Monans Harbour

At work on the *Harvest Moon* in St Monans harbour are D.Allan, J.Butters, D.Morris and J.Gowans. In the background is the *Paragon*, KY54.

St. Monans

In 1544, the English fleet entered St. Monans, captured the whole fishing fleet and burnt the town. They used the captured boats to land at Portobello, Leith and Newhaven. 200 years ago St. Monans had 35 boats of between 5 and 30 tons, but no harbour. Only a single jetty existed where the middle pier now stands. The boats, which were open decked with a single mast and dipping lug, measured between 16ft-40ft and were pulled up on a shingle beach.. From 1888 the local fleet consisted of 50 ft - 80 ft sailing Fifies.

From the *First Statistical Account* in the 1790's, it is obvious there were still arguments about the spelling of the town's name. The minister of the parish of Abercrombie gave a few different spellings and I have recently seen two St. Monans boats lying together in the harbour, with the home port name on one spelt 'St. Monance' and the other 'St. Monans'. As the latter seems to be in favour at present, that's the spelling I'll use in this chapter. From the *First Statistical Account:*

"With the last 5 years past the fish have deserted our seas (particularly the haddock). This is threatening an emigration of the population. The boats here number 14 large and 20 small, the small being used for the white fishing with a crew of five. The large boats are only used for the herring fishing with a crew of nine".

As for the *Second Statistical Account* by the Rev. Robert Swan, it says that fishing is the chief occupation in St Monans, giving work to 300 women baiting the lines. After a description of gear for the summer herring fishing of 26 boats, mainly headed for Caithness, the account mentions that the cod fishing is mainly for export, being sent mainly to London and Liverpool. Haddock, turbot and cod were sent to Edinburgh.

Since the sma' lines are more fully dealt with under the chapter on Pittenweem, we'll consider the beam trawl and its influence in this chapter.

In the *East of Fife Record*, June 6, 1890, there is an extract from a letter concerning the East Fife Fishing Industry, which states:

"The St. Monans fishermen were the first fishermen in Scotland to introduce the beam trawl and were experts on trawling. After complaints from Pittenweem and Cellardyke fishermen, a Royal Commission, with Huxley at its head, was appointed. He asked the St. Monans men why they trawled against the wishes of the Pittenweem and Cellardyke men. They replied that it paid them to do so as they could not catch rones and plaice flounders with a hook. Being asked what these fish feed on, the reply was "herring spawn". "How do you know?" they were asked. "Know man? Their stammachs are cake fou!" Huxley's report told them to trawl away. They were only stopped by a Pittenweem skipper dropping large stones on the smooth ground of the Traith."

Below you will see a drawing of the 'Thorean Stick', a tool used by the St Monans fishermen which was the equivalent of what the Dykers called a 'Gowking Iron', which was used to extract a hook which had been so well swallowed by the fish that the fishermen's hands would be damaged by extracting it.

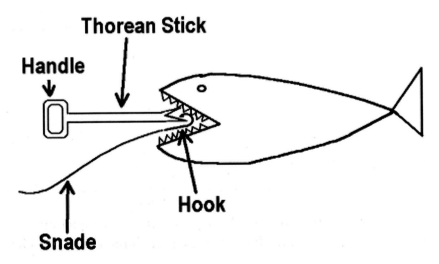

A wee touch of superstition now. I read Jack's *History of St. Monans* many years ago and took a note of some of the superstitions he mentioned. I am not going to mention many, as my friend who drew the Thorean stick for me made a quick reply on my teasing him about the superstitions of the St. Monans fishermen. Says he, "You Dykers are juist as bad." Says I, "you're quite right". I will tell you one superstition concerning the St Monans fishermen, and will even things up by telling one about the Dykers later. According to Jack, they tied on the hooks on their lines with scarlet thread. My friend denied it of course, but admitted he tied his on with white thread, whereas we simple Dykers tied them on with anything that was to hand.

I will now draw your attention to the number of boats in the 3 local burghs for 1914 (see tables at the rear of the book) and my arithmetic would put St. Monans ahead of the other two. Alas, today the Pittenweem total exceeds the other two and it's there you will find the local fish market now. I'm unsure as to how the market came to be situated at Pittenweem, but during my research I got permission from three of the Fishery Officers to look through old papers. I came across a complaint from Mr Aitken, a fish salesman from St. Monans, dated May 18, 1926. The complaint stated that:

"With exception of the years affected by the Great War, this is the first year landings of herring at St. Monans exceeded those at Anster. Usually, since the War, the fact is that a greater value of white fish is landed there".

The purpose of Mr Aitken's complaint was that he wanted the Fishery Officer to reside in St. Monans.

When the garret (attic) in the replica fisherman's house in the Fisheries Museum was being laid out, many items of gear which would have been stored in such a place was handed in by the local public. I had seen most of the items before, but I came across one I had never used, nor had my father. On enquiry I found it had been much used by the St. Monans men during the sailing boat days. It was called a 'drogue' and was used to slow the boat down to the required speed.

I should really close here, but I have just remembered something from my boyhood. My father's oldest brother Wull was drowned at the winter herring before I was born. He had been married to one of Scow's sisters, Scow being William Sutherland, last coxswain of the last sailing lifeboat in Anster. His widow went to Aberdeen to be a housekeeper to her brother, who had become a widower. He had a grandson called Benjie, who often accompanied her to Cellardyke on holiday. As he and I were of a similar age, I often accompanied them on their jaunts to visit relatives during their stay, including visits to her two married sisters in St. Monans.

One sister was married to a Gowans and the other married to a Mathers. When visiting 'Old Nance', who was Mrs. Gowans and lived, I think, in Miller Terrace, she said we would have to sit in the back room, so that she could see her doos (pigeons) coming in. "I'll hae to go," she suddenly said, then returned with a message she had taken from one of the pigeon's legs, sent from her husband who had been at the Sproules at the May Island. Reading the message, she said "They'll be hame in an hour". This was the only occasion when I saw the Pigeon Post in action in east Fife!

A Chronology of the Inshore Fishing Industry in St Monans from 1845 to 1952

The information has been taken mainly from the *Pittenweem Register* and the *East Fife Record*, with the dates quoted referring to the edition of the newspaper in question:

1845

June 14: A good number of fisher girls from St. Monans went to the sands of Ardross to gather sand eels. They created so much noise that they alarmed the inhabitants of Ardross, Abercrombie, Newark and Stenton. Each place sent an armed man to investigate, who fired volleys over the girls' heads. The girls were chased back to St. Monans, with the men firing an occasional shot. Torn garments could be seen on palings next day.

June 28: Price of haddocks at Leith last week was 5/- per 100. In Pittenweem, St. Monans and Cellardyke it was 2/6 per 120.

1846

June 24: Fishing boat *Margaret* of St. Monans lost at the line fishing, North West of the May Island. Five men were lost, with only the master, R. Tennant, saved by clinging to an oar.

July 11: A good many herring caught this week with 'jiggers'.

1847

Jan. 9: A St. Monans fisherman caught only 1 rone, a long lean, ill looking brute with only one eye. He shot his lines in Pithy's Ash Hole (close by the May).

Feb 4: A St. Monans boat was charged 6/- per 100 herring from a Buckhaven boat for bait. The following editions say little about St. Monans, the news being mainly about Anster and Pittenweem. Also, editions 52, 53 and 54 are missing from the library.

1855

Jan. 20: St. Monans' Baillie Innes got 20 score of cod on Saturday last. Fish merchant Tod paid out £100 for cod alone.

Feb 10: Large Cod landed at St. Monans, 56lb. weight, caught near May Island by W. Allan.

Sept. 21: Two men were hurt when the boats were being towed to the Moor at St. Monans. On Monday week Alan Watt caught 54 turbot and A. Danskin 28. Price 5/- per turbot.

Oct 19: St. Monans fishermen doing well at the May Island.

Dec.21: Mr. Scott, the owner of the *Pittenweem Register,* died on the 9th.

The place of the *Pittenweem Register* was filled by the *East Fife Record,* which lasted until 1916. Since it was owned by the Russell family, who lived in Anster, it is but natural that most of their news was about Anster. The first news about white fish appears to be general.

1857

May 30: 30 Boats landed 250 score of white fish, chiefly haddocks. The fish were caught by partially decked boats, fishing 70 miles out to sea. There were 8 men in each boat, each boat having shot 15 taes of 120 hooks each.

1868

Haddock fishing closed. It was a poor year and, from then on, only general statements were made about the fishing industry until:

1872

Jan 12: 12 St. Monans boats trawling in the Traith for halibut and plaice (a subject which was to cause argument between Pittenweem and St. Monans for some time).

1874

Jan 30: St. Monans boats trying trawl, unprecedented at this time of year.

1877

Aug 31: Beam trawling was forbidden in the Traith for 3 years from 1862.

No improvement in fish stocks resulted from this restriction so it was cancelled.

1890

June 6: St. Monans fishermen were the first in Scotland to introduce the beam trawl. They said rones and plaice fed on herring spawn. Huxley's report said, "trawl away". They were only stopped by a Pittenweem fisherman dropping large stones in the Traith.

1897

Apr. 9: Haddock yawls at Pittenweem and St. Monans sold haddocks at 7/- to 9/- per box.
Their catches varied from 1° to 5 boxes.

1899

Feb. 9: Value of all kinds of fish landed for January:

	1899	1898
Anstruther	£3,289	£1,690
Pittenweem	319	540
St. Monans	810	689
Crail and Kingsbarns	119	287
Totals for District	£5,513	£4,227

Apr.14: Improved catches by St. Monans haddock yawls (mainly of cod).

1904

May 27: Current fishing industry statistics for St. Monans: 100 boats, 372 resident fishermen and 204 non-resident.

1906

Jan 26: Pittenweem and St. Monans have 59 boats and bauldies employed at the sma' lines.

1910

Miller launched a yawl for Arbroath, measuring 27ft by 10ft.

1911

Nov. 2: Miller to build 28ft. motor yawl for J. Davidson of St. Monans.

1912

Sept. 5: St. Monans boats reported to be the best fished of the local fleets at the drave.

1913

May20: Miller installed 15 hp Kelvin into *Spero Meliora* (A. Irvine) 38° ft, speed 6∫ miles per hour.

July 10: Two 30ft motor boats launched at St. Monans by W. Reekie, bound for Arbroath.

Oct. 19: W. Reekie launched a yawl at St Monans, the *Bird*, for J. Bowman, Calman's Wynd. Dimensions 28° ft. by 10 ft.

1914

In St. Monans there are now 9 fishing yawls between 36ft and 41ft in length fitted with 15 hp. Kelvin engines, all by Miller.

Apr. 30: At St. Monans, 11 boats currently being fitted with motor engines, of which 7 are for St. Monans, 3 for Pittenweem and 1 for Crail. The St. Monans fleet for the summer fishing will number 109 vessels.

Sept. 4: Inshore line fishermen to send cargoes to Glasgow.

1915

Jan 21: Line fishing to be allowed within ° mile of low water mark from vessels under 35 ft.

May 6: Yawl *Sunbeam,* 29° ft by 10ft 8", built at St Monans for R. Cargill, Anstruther. Fitted with a 15 hp Kelvin engine.

1916

Jan 15: Great Line fishing records broken at St. Monans.

1917

30 yawls fishing from St. Monans within 1 mile of shore.

Feb. 22: Cod net fishing very successful, landings 7-11 score per boat. This is the first mention of cod nets. Fish mainly sold at Pittenweem at 5/- to 8/6 each for prime cod. Fulton of Pittenweem launched a 40ft Bauldie fitted with a 30 hp. Kelvin for Jas. Wood of St. Monans, named *Julia Wood.*

Oct. 4: On Monday, 6 Motor boats from St. Monans and 1 from Anster left for the south
accompanied by the usual convoy.

1918

Oct. 24: Flu epidemic in east Fife.

Nov. 7: All schools closed.

Nov 14: The end of the First World War: news of peace reached the district after midday on Monday.

Nov 28: Last Thursday forenoon in bright sunshine, double lines of British ships with the German Fleet between them sailed up the Firth. Some anchored in Largo Bay, others near Inchkeith.

1919

Feb. 21: Fair supplies of whitefish.

March 27: Fishermen's big earnings enticing men over 70 to go back to sea after being retired.

April 3: More whitefish landed.

May 1: Treasury to sell 400 trawlers and drifters built during the war for active service.

July 24: Peace Day celebrated last Saturday. A beacon was lit on Kellie Law.

July 31: Anster and Cellardyke fishermen on strike.

Sept. 18: Fishermen's strike ended.

Sept. 25: 70 Cellardyke fishermen reported to be working in St. Monans boats.

Dec 4: 30 St Monans pupils attending navigation class.

1920

Jan 15: St. Monans reports good catches of cod from cod nets.
Feb. 26: 250 cwt. of whitefish valued at £580 landed in the district.

1922

Jan 5: More fish landed at St Monans than there had been for years, selling at £6-£11 per score.
April 20: All St. Monans boats employed at the great lines, one boat reporting catches worth £150 during the previous week.

1923

Jan 4: Good landings of white fish at St. Monans last Friday, with war-time prices realised.

1924

Feb 7: *Vigilant* (T. Adam) and *Children's Friend* (J. Hutt) landed ringed herrings caught farther up the Firth. Cellardyke fishermen decided no more to be landed at Anster, a move which was supported by buyers.

1925

Feb.2:. Good prices for whitefish at St. Monans.

1926

Sept.16: Best drave since the War. 48 St. Monans vessels (compared with 104 in 1916) averaged £1,100 per boat.

1927

Jan 13: Some Pittenweem and St. Monans bauldies fishing at Rothesay.
Jan 27: St. Monans bauldies home from Rothesay after successful season.
Feb. 17: Considerable quantity of white fish landed at St. Monans. Large supplies of skate.
May 30: *Orion* launched at Anster for A. Doig of Cellardyke. Dimensions 49ft. 9in. by 15ft. 6 in. by 5ft 6in.
Dec 2: *Protect Me III,* with 45 hp Kelvin engine installed, built by Reekie for R. Marr.

KY171 *Celtic* at the Middle Pier, St Monans

KY134 *Girl Christian* in St Monans harbour

Packing fish in David Gerrard's fish shed, St Monans, 1960 (Cowie Collection)

KY118 *Orion II* in St Monans

72

1928

<u>Feb 16:</u> Good catches of cod fetching £3 to £6-18/- per score.

<u>Aug 4:</u> Arbroath boat *Ben Venuto* launched at St. Monans, measuring 49ft by 16ft with a 48hp Gardner engine.

<u>Aug 9:</u> Miller launched *Nil Desperandum* for Campbeltown, measuring 46ft by 14ft. Seven years ago he built the first 'canoe sterned' boat for Campbeltown.

<u>Oct. 4:</u> *Clan MacKay* launched at St. Monans by Reekie, measuring 66ft by 17ft. The engine was a 72 hp semi-direct diesel, specially designed for use on the Forth and Clyde Canal (through which the smaller boats gained access to the west coast). This was the first Fifie launched for 20 years.

1929

<u>March 28</u>: Notable absence of St. Monans news.

<u>Oct 3</u>: *Shenendoah*, measuring 48ft by 14°ft with a 36hp Kelvin engine launched. Bound for Campbeltown.

1930

<u>Jan 2</u>: Good catches of white fish.

<u>Jan 9 & Jan 16</u>: St. Monans cod fetching £6 per score.

<u>Jan 30:</u> 4 score cod landed. Best shot 70/- to 100/- per score.

<u>Feb 13</u>: St. Monans fishermen boycott ring net. Two 'nobbies', *Faustina* and *Mary Campbell,* were chased out of St. Monans.

1931

<u>April 30</u>: St. Monans men accuse Pittenweem men of doing damage to herring spawn with cod nets. The Pittenweem fishermen contend that during the 15 years the nets have been in use, the herring here have been plentiful. More poaching in Forth by seine net fishermen of Cockenzie and Port Seton.

<u>June 4</u>: 200 Cooneyites visit St. Monans. They do this every year and baptize in the open sea.

<u>Nov 19</u>: *Casimir* sunk at Yarmouth.

<u>Dec. 31</u>: *Enterprise,* 36ft fitted with 30hp Kelvin engine, built for Aitken and McKay of Pittenweem by W. Reekie.

1932

March 3: School Roll: Waid Academy 343, Cellardyke 386, St. Monans 211, Pittenweem 188 Crail 199, Elie 97.

1933

Jan 12: St. Monans bauldies employed at the great lines.

Apr 19: *Kingfisher* launched. Length 48 ft. and fitted with a 66hp Kelvin Diesel, built by W. Reekie for A. Robertson of Campbeltown.

May 6: Motor Ambulance for east Fife.

Oct. 26: *Floreat II,* measuring 51ft by 16ft powered by an 88hp engine launched by Reekie at St.Monans.

Nov23: 18 out of 19 St. Monans boats home from Yarmouth. Only 9 vessels cleared expenses.

Dec 7: *White Heather II* launched by Miller for T. Gay. Dimensions 50ft by 16ft.

1934

Jan 4: *June Rose,* 50ft by 16ft with an 85hp Gardner Diesel launched at St. Monans for W. Smith of Arbroath.

Jan 11: St. Monans boat *Girl Mina* lost 10 cod nets over the weekend.

Jan 18: Cod fetching £6 per score at St. Monans.

Jan 25: Good catches of white fish reported at St. Monans.

Feb. 1: St. Monans boats report good catches at great lines.

Aug. 23: St Monans fishermen W. Reekie and A. Reekie lost overboard off Peterhead.

Aug. 30: No assistance for bauldies in Government scheme.

Oct. 4: Death of Sir Ralph Anstruther.

1935

Jan 10 & Jan 24: St. Monans reports good supplies of Great Line fish

Jan 31: Good prices for Great Line fish at St. Monans.

Nov. 21: St. Monans fishermen J. Tarvit and W. Innes drowned from M.B. *Sunshine.*

1936

Jan 16: Most St. Monans boats reported to be working the Great Lines with good results.

March 26: *Courageous II* launched by Reekie for the Wilson family. Dimensions 46ft by 15ft and fitted with a 36HP engine.

April 16: Third Amateur International cap for W. Peattie of St Monans.

May 21: St. Monans Swifts F.C. ended the season with 6 trophies and only two defeats. W. Peattie signed for Raith Rovers.

May 28 *Argosy* launched by Reekie for Alan Lawson. Length 53 ft. with an 80hp National engine.

1937

Jan 14: Good catches of line fish.

Jan 21: Good catches of line fish. Pittenweem storm booms on.

Jan 28: £3,213 grant for St. Monans harbour. Keen demand for great line fish at St. Monans.

Sept. 19: Anster steam drifters berthed in St. Monans because of the coffer dam at Anstruther harbour.

1938

Jan 4: St Monans man Robert Reekie passed First Mate Foreign Going Certificate in Glasgow.

Jan 13: Good landings of white fish at St. Monans. A few boxes sold at 12/6 per box.

February 3: Keen demand for white fish at St Monans.

No fishing news reported for St. Monans in **1939**.

1940

Light catches from great line fishing at St Monans.

Jan 18: Provost Gourlay for Kirkcaldy.

February 15: W. P. Miller new Provost of St. Monans.

March 16: Death of the Earl of Crawford at Wigan, aged 69 years.

No fishing news reported for St. Monans in **1941, 1942, 1943** and **1944**.

1945

May 10: V.E. (Victory in Europe) celebrated.
June 7: Resignation of Provost Miller.
July 12: Baillie Guthrie succeeds Provost Miller.
July 24: Retiral of Dr. Wilson.
August 16: Surrender of Japan.

1946

Jan 3: Chlorination of water supply to continue.
February 23: Cockenzie boat *Thrive* sunk by explosion between the May Island and the Bass Rock. Two men were lost.
Mar 21: All fishermen to be included in the new Insurance Act.
April 18: 48 east Fife boats have been sold.
June 27: *Vigilant II* launched at Anster for James Adam of St. Monans.
Nov. 28: *Good Design II,* measuring 50ft and powered by an 88HP Kelvin engine, launched at St. Monans for Watson and Wood.
Dec. 12: *Golden Arrow,* dimensions 54 ft. by 17˚ ft with an 88HP Kelvin diesel, launched by Miller for Provost Carstairs.
Dec. 19: St Monans goes wet.

1947

Jan 2: Local herring producers and white fish producers agree to bury the hatchet.
Jan 9: Fishing fleet storm bound with mountainous seas and a south-easterly gale. Structural damage to St Monans houses reported.
Feb. 13: New slipway proposed for St. Monans.
Feb. 20: Roadmen exhausted working 16 hours per day attempting to clear the roads. The conditions are said to be the worst for 50 years. 100 men from the Labour Exchange and 50 German prisoners made 5 attempts to get from St. Andrews to Largoward and all failed. The District Nurse took 4 hours to make a 2 mile journey to Largoward through the fields to a confinement. Mrs. Elder had a son.
February 27: Weather turned bad again, with the road between Anster and St. Monans blocked.
March 26: 160 men relieved Peat Inn on Sunday. Six students on skis

visited isolated farms and brought back information.

May 22: *Shepherd Lad* launched at St. Monans for the Dunn family.

June 12: First charge since St. Monans went wet.

1948

Jan 1: 4 launches at St. Monans: *New Dawn*, length 50ft, built by Reekie for Pittenweem; *John*, length 50 ft, built by Miller and bound for the Hebridies; *Mary McMaster* built by Miller for Ireland and *Stardust*, length 52 ft, built by Reekie for Fisheron.

Jan. 8: Fishermen to get full benefit under N.H.S. Bill in July.

Feb 19: W. Reekie launched 2 boats, 1 for Ireland and 1 for Hopeman.

Feb 26: Reekie launched 50 ft. boat for Buckie at Anster. Fisheries Research Vesssel *Clupea* to investigate slump in average Forth catches.

Mar 25: On Tuesday *Clupea* had 16 herring (her biggest catch had been 30 herring).

April 15: Article relating to Miller's Bicentenary.

1949

Feb. 10: *Vigilant* of St. Monans sold to Ireland.

Oct. 27: Boatbuilder W. Reekie died following a fall. He left £37,000.

1950

Feb. 16: Smith and Aitken bought Reekie's boat building yard.

1951

Feb. 8: *Hope* and *Good Design* reverted to line fishing.

May 3: St. Monans' J. Ritchie capped for Scottish Schoolboys at football.

Aug 30: Death of Aitken, boatbuilder.

1952

Feb. 14: Proclamation of Queen.

Mar 11: P. Gay to play at Wembley.

April 24: J. Braid named as Provost of St. Monans.

The East Pier at Buckhaven in the early 1900's. Note the leather sea boots worn by the fisherman standing second right.

Buckhaven Harbour in the early 1900's

From Elie around Largo Bay to Methil

Elie (and Earlsferry)

The *First Statistical Account* says very little about Elie's Fishing industry. According to the account, there were five fishermen living rent-free in houses belonging to Sir John Anstruther, on the condition they supplied the Elie people with fish at least 3 times a week. On the whole, they were pretty successful. Like all citizens of the east Fife coast, including scholars from St. Andrews, they took part in the Lammas Drave in the 1850's and 1860's but, after the First World War, there was only one fisherman actively engaged in the fishing and, as in all the other creeks, a few part timers during the summer.

Largo

The Parish boundary of Largo includes two and a half miles of sea coast, but as this is the only fishing village between Buckhaven and St. Andrews where I have no acquaintances or personal sources of information, we'll firstly refer to the *First Statistical Account*, from 1791-99:

"Ten years ago fish abounded on this coast, particularly haddock of a very delicate kind. But since that period fish of every kind have been scarce, insomuch that there is not a haddock in the bay. All that remains are a few small cod, podlies and flounders. The fishermen have also disappeared, who 20 years ago, were the chief inhabitants of Largo and Drummochy. At present there is not a fisherman in Largo and only one in Drummochy who fishes in summer and catches rabbits in winter".

The *Second Statistical Account*, 1840-45, has less information:

"Some years ago a salmon stake net fishery was commenced in Largo Bay. The rent was one fourteenth of the gross product. The annual amount of

fish sold on an average of 5 years was only £130 and from expenses nearly half of the capital was lost. The undertaking has been resumed, and is now more prosperously carried on".

The account also states that a steam boat plies twice a day in summer and once in winter between Largo and Newhaven, but doesn't say what it carries. That is about all the information remotely concerned with fishing (dated 1837).

The *Third Statistical Account*, published in 1952 by Alex Smith, says that mixed arable farming is the main industry in the Largo area. About 1890, an Edinburgh club applied for permission to lay out a golf course along the shore. Negotiations with the proprietor did not succeed, which seems a pity (even more so today with the closure of the railway). For long the principal occupation of the men in the coastal port of the parish was fishing and Largo Bay figures in a number of Fife fishing songs. But the fish have now left the bay, in the opinion of many local people, because of the trawlers which used to be seen frequently in the area. The last commercial fishing boat was sold in 1948, and lobsters and salmon fishing have also ceased now. The Largo-Newhaven steamer service is also a thing of the past.

One feature, however, is the number of fish hawkers who still operate from the town, carrying their wares in vans over a considerable distance. Many of them are descended from the former fishing population.

The only reference to the Largo fishing industry I have been able to find in the *East of Fife Record* is from March 3rd 1899, when it is stated that the Largo fishermen send plaice direct to the market in order to cut out middle-men.

Just one story about Largo. My father's last year at the creels was 1947 and one day he told me to take his lobsters along to Burgon's, the shellfish merchant. It happened to be old Martin Sutherland on duty, who asked me what was the biggest lobster I had ever caught. "A six pounder" I replied. "Come and see this", he said, and showed me a big one. "What weight is it?" I asked. "Nine pounds and a quarter", replied Martin. It lay perfectly still, unable to lift its huge claws. "Where did it come from?" I enquired. "Lergie" he said.

Methil

Methil was not regarded by the fisher folk of the East Neuk as a place where you sold fish, but rather as the place that the steam fishing boats went to for coal after the 1926 strike or as the home town of East Fife Football Club. It was cheaper, even, for the Aberdeen trawlers to come to Methil for coal, than to have it delivered by train, so there was a regular traffic of Aberdeen trawlers past the villages of the East Neuk.

In the extreme poverty of the thirties, many of the east Fife fishermen transferred to Aberdeen and remained there. Those who had left relatives in the East Neuk got into the habit of blowing their whistle in different patterns as they passed by, so that their relatives might recognise them as they made their way up to Methil for coal. One Sunday morning, on a beautiful summers day, the people at the Cellardyke bathing pool saw one of their ex-townsmen come closer in to shore than he ever dared again, as the spectators distinctly heard him hit the rocks we knew as the 'Outer Yard'. It's a skelly that never breaks the water, but causes the sea to break over it when the tide is out, in the middle of a South Easterly gale.

I remember going up to Methil for coal and being greeted by some East Neuk men who worked for Matthew Taylor the coal merchant. One was a Doig, who had played for the Bluejackets, the old Cellardyke football team. "Watch him", said my father, "He's very supple". But I took my eyes off him and, next thing I knew, he was standing beside me. He had made standing leap from the pier to the boat and was down on the hold hatches beside us. My father said he never touched the deck! One of the other men my father knew had the same name as us and was married to an East Neuk woman. Their son was also Pete Smith and I had the pleasure of meeting the family one Sunday whilst out walking the Lade Braes at St. Andrews of all places. Together we made four Pete Smiths, as there was also a grandson present.

For several years, especially since the demise of Buckhaven harbour, small yawls have been berthed alongside the wooden piers which form the entrance channel to Methil No.3 Dock. The boats are used mainly by local men who, in their spare time, fish for codlings or mackerel using handlines.

Some of the yawls are also used for creel fishing.

Recent years have seen some prawn boats berthing on the north side of the entrance channel to No.3 Dock. One of the main reasons for the boats using Methil as a base is that the entrance channel is deep enough to be unaffected by tide levels, which means the moorings are accessible at all times. There is no local market for their catch, however, and the boats either land at Pittenweem or transport their catch to the market by road. As for the history of the Methil fishing industry, you'll find all I know on page 34 of *Maritime Methil* by G. J. Downie and M. Cameron, in which they mention a few boats, only five of them having ML numbers. The *Iris* and *Maggie Deas* were mentioned, but only because they were using Methil after Buckhaven harbour was ruined. They also mention the preference of the Buckhaven fleet for fishing from North Shields, which was well known in east Fife. As for Leven I know even less, and the port is certainly not mentioned in any maritime almanac that I have ever seen.

Recent years have seen small prawn boats use the wooden pier alongside the former entrance channel to Methil No.3 dock as a base

Buckhaven

As the Buckhaven fleet diminished due to the influence of the neighbouring coal pits, which could employ men at a steady wage, the names of the Buckhaven boats gradually disappeared from the fishermen's Almanacs as they restricted their information to vessels of 15 tons or more.

Several years ago, Miss Deas, a Buckhaven woman, was visiting Capt. Keir's widow in Elie. Capt. Keir came from Wemyss and Mrs. Keir came from Buckhaven, and I was invited along to meet Miss Deas as she had a friend, a daughter of William Taylor of Buckhaven, who remembered my father. She had met my father nearly 70 years ago when he fished out of Buckhaven, during which time he became very friendly with the two Taylor brothers, who had a motor yawl named the *Iris*, ML345.

The *Iris* was not mentioned in the Buckhaven fishing fleet of 1918, but appears in the 1926, 1930, 1940 and 1947 almanacs. The owners, T. Taylor & W. Taylor, are mentioned in the list of Buckhaven boats in 1914 as the partners in the *Isabella*. They were great friends of my father's and used to come down to Anster during the 1930's to fish for herring at the anchor nets. I used to like to go to Tam's house, where the mother addressed her sons as Robert, William and Thomas. I didn't know whether that was the fashion or not. I used to see Tam Taylor with one of his sons, who brought him along to see the steam drifters. He was also the cousin of James Taylor (Taggie), who was the salesman here during the winter herring and, if they were selling outside, his voice could be heard over half the harbour. Tam & Willie worked the sma' lines in the *Iris*, as John Deas did in the *Maggie Deas*. The boat was named after his daughter Maggie Deas who emigrated to America, and when I had the great pleasure of meeting her on her last visit home, she told me how she had often passed the house where I lived in West Forth Street, Cellardyke on her visit to meet a friend to go dancing, when all the fish buyers were here. Alas, she has passed on as well as her friend old Mrs. Keir, whom she was visiting. They were two very vivacious old ladies. I asked Mrs. Keir where her husband belonged. "The Wemyss, Same place as Capt. Moodie", she said, "the first Master of the *Cutty Sark*".

She said she used to go to visit Capt. Moodie and his wife when he had retired to Methil. He had a mast erected in his garden, on which he hoisted his flag in the morning and took it down at night. Capt. Moodie was chosen to overlook the building of the *Cutty Sark*, as well as to be first Captain. He worked with the designer, Hercules Linton, who had a great admiration for the Firth of Forth fishing boats, which were famed throughout the Kingdom of Fife for their speed and sea worthiness.

In moulding together the best points of the old clipper *Tweed*, and the Buckhaven fishing boats, Hercules Linton became a supremely successful ship designer. Further information on this subject can be seen on page 23 of *Log of the Cutty Sark* by Lubbock.

Information regarding Buckhaven fishermen and fishermen from the two Wemyss harbours, taken from the *First Statistical Account*, states:

"for the scarcity of haddocks for some years, several of the fishermen have entered the navy or merchant ships and others are day labourers. Formerly East Wemyss had 5 boats, each with 5 men. West Wemyss had 1 boat with 5 men. Now only 1 boat in East Wemyss, and the crew are all old men. About 40 years ago, there were 25,000 haddocks landed in one day, sold at 6d. to 10d. per 100, now more is sometimes given for a single haddock. Today most of the fish are sent to Edinburgh, the remainder are sold in the neighbourhood by women. 12 boats with 6 men in each crew used to go to Dunbar in August, but abandoned it after poor returns. They marry when young, mainly to local women."

Less information is given in the *Second Statistical Account*, which states that the local area employed 170 men at the fishing, all residing in Buckhaven. They have 124 fishing boats of various dimensions. The report then goes on to mention 1st class boats numbering 60, each boat valued at £75, 2nd class boats, 42 valued at £40 and 3rd class boats numbering 40 at £14 each. I hadn't heard about 3rd class boats before, so I had to look elsewhere for further information. This I found in a copy of the *Pittenweem Register*. Naturally, most of the news is local, mainly concerning Pittenweem, but the following article, entitled The Buckers, appeared on

84

Tam Taylor on the *Isabella's* with his daughter. He was later to own a motor yawl ML345 *Iris* with his brother Willie.

The Buckhaven sma' line boat ML359 *Maggie Deas*, owned by John Deas and named after his daughter, who had emigrated to America.

KY505 *Gratti* in Buckhaven Harbour. This was one of the last fishing boats to be built in Buckhaven, by local boatbuilder David Brown.

22 August 1846:

"The Buckhaven fishermen seem to take up their encampment on the sea at the very commencement of the herring fishing. Look out what time you will and you will surely see the Buckers on the water. They are like the planets. They never tire or stop or rest. When one eye is shut in sleep, the other is wide awake watching the fish. They require no lodging - their boat is their nest night and day during the drave. All work and no play is a Buckerman's joy, but all work and no play makes a Pittenweemer a bad boy. The Buckers have the character of being of a persevering disposition very careful of their earnings and have their boats right well appointed with everything requisite for their calling. Many of them have money saved".

From a book by Frank Rankin, *Auld Buckhyne Revisited*, I got the following information about Buckhaven boat builders:

<u>Mungo Baird:</u> Built fishing boats on the west sands from 1877-90, when he went to Muiredge to make pit props.

<u>David Brown:</u> His last two boats were *Gratti* and *Empress*. Each vessel was 52 ft. in length and cost £200. Giving the length is most important as giving the tonnage merely results in guess work as to whether they are seine or line boats or gartlin or drave boats.

As for Buckhaven harbour, when my father was up there about 1930, the redd from the Wellesley Pit was already beginning to silt up the harbour. The above book mentions 1937 as the date when the harbour first started to crumble, when a storm made a break of 30-40 yards in the east pier. At this time only about 5 boats used the harbour. The break widened until the lighthouse finally collapsed during a storm in 1942, by which time the few remaining boats were either working from Methil or West Wemyss. A number of years ago I decided to take a look at the harbour and my wife and I walked along the beach from east to west until we came to it. I talked to some men beside a hut and asked for Tam Taylor of the *Iris*. I was told he was in good health and he would probably come down to the harbour later on, but we never saw him on our return. I was able to walk from the east pier right across to the west pier and let my wife see where the old *Day Dawn* used to tie-up when my father worked there at the creels with Eckie Reid and James Watson (Patchie).

They caught a lot of lobsters and partans whilst fishing from Buckhaven. Patchie said that when they hauled a fleet of creels near Methil Docks, they were 'sitting looking at you like cats'.

Crail fishermen George and Sandy Meldrum with their Uncle Sandy

Creel Fishing in the East Neuk

It is difficult to know which is the earliest source of our shellfish industry's history. I will mention three.

Gourlay's book *Memorials of Cellardyke*, published in 1879; *The First Statistical Survey of Fife*, 1799; and an article from the *East of Fife Record* in 1869, telling the story of an old fisherman aged 84. Gourlay's book mentions that on some unknown date in the past when herring were scarce in the spring months, the cod and ling fishers who preferred herring as bait, baited their big hooks with crab or partan. The crabs were fished for in rotation by one of the crew, working the creels while the boats were at sea. His other mentions of lobsters were obviously taken from the *First Statistical Account* of 1799, so we will quote directly from it:

"Nothing about shellfish from Anster Easter; but Anster Wester said that lobsters were the only fish sent to London"

The lobsters were presumably sent by boat from Leith before the railways came to Edinburgh in 1848. It was supposed that about £1,000 was annually brought into the area from the lobster trade. Pittenweem also said they sent a considerable amount of lobster to London, but the Parish of Kilrenny, which included Cellardyke, made no mention of them, neither did St. Monans. Crail, however, as would be expected, did mention lobsters. They said that "20-25 thousand lobsters are sent every year to the London market", and that 10 years previously there had been double that number.

It said that six boats were at the white or cod fishing and six smaller boats at the lobster fishing. I mentioned earlier a third source of information from the East Fife Record about an old fishermen of 84. He said that at the age of 12 he went with three other persons in a yawl owned by John Watt of Anster Customs House, who paid more attention to his Custom duties than the state of the tide, so he left him for a noted crab fisher named James

Boyter. At that time there was no market for partans, the usual catch being 4-6 dozen from about 20 creels which was the utmost number of creels fished by a yawl, lack of bait being the restrictive factor in the size of the fleet.

The article continued by saying they couldn't exactly say when partans became marketable, but they thought that old Thomas Murray was the first to attempt to get a market, sometime before 1800, when he bought up some crabs, boiled them, and sailed up the Tay to Perth where he sold them. The price he sold the cooked crabs for was never known, and this helped to exaggerate the success of his venture. The next year, Fisherrow and Prestonpans yawls that came down to the 'couping' of white fish, also offered 4d. per dozen for good saleable crabs, and so started a new era in the fishing. The 'couping' was a method which evolved by boats from some of the fishing villages near Edinburgh coming across to the outlying vil-lages on the Fife coast, buying cheap and selling dear in Edinburgh, rather than fishing themselves. The date offered for this was about 1809. We have thus arrived at the period when crabs became marketable as an article of food, disposed of by women, as far as they could carry them for 4d. a dozen. The next mention is of John Neilson from Ceres who offered 6d. per dozen of 13, which price after Whitsunday was reduced to 5d per dozen.

Breaking away from the article about the old man, whose name, alas, is never mentioned, the *Second Statistical Account*, dated 1841, only men-tions partans and lobsters under Crail, who fished with 12 boats.
They sent 4,000 lobsters to London in 1840, and 3,000-4,000 dozen crabs to Dundee and Edinburgh.

The previous article now takes us on to 1845 and after, when Mr. Strachan, a London agent, raised the price to 7d. per dozen for partans and lobsters at 6d. each. The arrival of the train to Edinburgh in 1848, and to Anster in 1863, was the next major change, the first date seeing the arrival of George Thomson and Mr. Addy from England, bringing with them some real competition. This raised the prices as high as 1/6d per dozen for crabs (the same as we got in the 1930's) before settling down to a price of about one shilling per dozen. By the way, Mr. Addy's bell is in the possession of the

Painting the Crail creel boat ML275 *Be in Time,* owned by J. Watson

The Crail boat *Be in Time* KY3 about to enter Crail Harbour. This was not the same *Be in Time* seen in the first photograph, which was a clinker built vessel as opposed to the carvel design of the boat in the second photograph. KY3 *Be in Time* was owned by R. Watson, son of the owner of ML275 *Be in Time.*

Crail fisherman Harry Smith pictured with a young crew member

Harry Smith in the process of extracting shellfish from his creels

Fisheries Museum, and was used to call the buyers to auctions right up to the end of the winter herring fishing. So concluded the article of 1869 in the *East Fife Record*, called 'Crab fishing past and present'.

You may read a generalisation of the above in Gourlay's book, where he mentions a schoolboy liking for wulks and partan taes, and getting a dozen partan taes for a penny before the days of the 'iron horse'.

The *Pittenweem Register* existed from 1844 - 1855, so I combed through all the available copies searching for information about the local shellfish industry with very little result. However, there was a mention on October 24th, 1846, about Pittenweem periwinkles (known here as wulks, not to be confused with whelks, which are larger):

"We have had occasion more than once to notice new sources of wealth springing up in our Royal Burgh, and the present one, though rather diminutive in appearance, is making more noise among the juvenile nobility in London that our far-famed Pittenweem coal would do in that quarter when it is in full operation. The young Prince, it is said, has a dish of them every day and we may soon expect to hear of a London shellfish monger having over his stall 'Purveyor of Pittenweem Periwinkles to H.R.H. the Prince of Wales".

The next mention of crabs after the 1869 article in the *East Fife Record* is in 1875, when it gave a warning to the crab fishers here who were not restricted to any size, but all above half size were sold at two shillings per dozen and small at 6d. per dozen. The warning was about selling the small ones, and said that Cromer had brought in a bye-law limiting the sale of crabs to a minimum of four and a half inches across the back. It wasn't long before the Government acted and in 1877 the Oyster, Crab and Lobster Act was passed, which said lobsters must measure eight inches from the tip of the beak to the end of the tail, and the crabs must be four and a quarter inches across the back. So it remained until 1914 when the measurement for the crabs became four and a half inches. Beadwell, in Northumberland, seemed to be the main research station of the scientists and, in the local paper dated March 30, 1906, it mentioned how a marked crab had been recaptured having walked 108 miles in 114 days. Another liberated in March was re-caught off Kincardineshire, 80 miles distant, in July.

Before leaving the period prior to the First World War, I will mention an article which appeared in 1906 describing Crail crab fishing. It described the bait used, viz. cod heads and coalfish. Fresh bait was used for partans, but not necessarily so for lobsters. The depth of water in which they fished was from six to twelve fathoms. The article closes with a sentence which will please my Crail friends: "Crail crabs are considered finer than those from any other part of the coast".

During the First World War few statistics were given, but in May 1916 Crail dispatched by train 59 bags of wulks in one week and 56 the next week, so it would appear some restrictions were applied to the partan and lobster fishing. The year 1919 saw the first mention of post-war activity in the shellfish industry, when it was stated that 12 yawls were employed in lobster fishing in August, with catches ranging from 18 to 60 lobsters per day. In 1923, however, there was a sign that all was not going well in the fishing industry in general when, in November, the local paper said that so many bags of wulks were mailed daily, the beds must be almost bare.

Following a couple of poor fishing seasons in succession, half the men in the local towns would be gathering wulks at the seaside. By 1931 the Crail fishermen objected to details of the partan fishing being published and after that very little information was made available. There were good catches of crabs at Crail in 1938, the first hard news of an improvement in partan fishing as we experienced a near famine of crabs in the mid-thirties when they were all said to be walking north.

I said "we", as I was employed for most summers from the mid-twenties as a crew member with my father in our yawls during holidays from my educational studies, both as schoolboy and student.

More orders have been promulgated about restrictions on landing size of crabs and lobsters in the last 40 years than in the previous 80 years. One change in 1951 saw the crabs still the same, with their minimum of four and a half inches across the back, but the lobster length had to be not less than nine inches and no lobster carrying the spawn was to be sold. This lasted until 1976 when the new restriction order was given in metric num bers: (a) Crabs to be not less than 115 mm across the back, which is just above four and a half inches; (b) Lobsters were to be not less than 80 mm measured along the carapace from the rear of the eye socket to the rear end of the body shell.

In 1986 an Act prohibited the landing of crab claws alone, but now the fisherman had to cut the moving part of the claw, so they could no longer bite. They then have to be kept in boxes in the sea until the cut part partially heals, otherwise they appear to die. The most up to date law appeared in 1993, increasing the restriction in size from 80 mm to 85 mm.

My personal involvement with partans starts at a very early age, during the winter herring season of 1919 when I was four. Although I had tasted partans at home by this time, this was the first time I remember being on a fishing boat. She was a sailing bauldie between 35-40 ft. named the *Glad Tidings* and owned by the Watson family of Cellardyke, who had both sailing boats and steam drifters named *Pride of Fife*. The boat was on loan to Jeck Dick, and the rest of the crew were W. Gardner, A. Thomson and my father. I believe they fished well, prices being high just after the war. The boat was lying near the end of the east pier and I don't know how I got on board, as the tide was nearly fully out. They had a good shot of herring and lots of cod out of the cod nets. I remember sitting on the sail watching them unwinding their catch and, when they had finished, their fry to take home consisted of a codlin' each and some partans. This was not the only fishing action that affected my life as well as many others that same year. My father told me a little about it, but I got more information from others as I grew up. Father came in from the sea to find that the crews had gone on strike against the skippers, claiming they were getting fewer shares than in the other fishing ports in East Scotland. My father, who didn't call the strike, was however elected to the strike committee and became their spokesman. After about 11 weeks, the fishermen won, or at least the skippers lost. This had a serious side effect on my father and other members of the strike committee as he found it difficult to get a berth in a drifter fishing out of Anster and often had recourse to going in Pittenweem and St. Monans boats, as these ports had kept clear of the strike. This so upset my uncle, the only one in the family with money, that he bought my father an

18 ft. sailing yawl, so that he need no longer go out of the town to get a job. From the age of nine or ten, I was brought up in yawls which spent part of the year at the creels. Before he got his own yawl, my father went for a summer in a yawl named the *Janet*, ML67, owned by A. E. Reid, and it was in this boat I saw my first creel hauled. Although father left one or two diaries, there is no mention of her, and I know I was still at primary school when he got his first yawl, which he named the *Ivy*, KY 151. She came from Boddam, where my mother hailed from, and that started me off on a career of creel fishing extending for nearly 30 years. He had been preparing for the arrival of the yawl by making creels and his chief tutor was Jock Deas, with whom he had gone to the winter herring both before and after the First World War.

Jock told him not to try to make his creels one at a time, as it was a soul destroying experience. He said he had once tried it, starting at 7 a.m. and only stopping for meals, but he had not completed it by 7 p.m. We had a day in the country looking for creel boughs, ash preferred as there were fewer unsuccessful attempts at bending them into a semi-circle, after steaming them across a washing boiler, which most houses had outside at the back. We were, of course, forced to take other trees, like gean and dog rose. The strongest were supposed to be 'Whun Rits' (Whin Roots), not really the roots, but young branches. This we gave up as breakages were too high, but the few boughs I did see made from 'Whun Rits' were extremely strong. Wooden barrel hoops in pairs were also used, but willow was no use as they tapered away too soon. You bent as many boughs as you could, tied them across in a semi-circular state, and stowed them away. All the time you were making the netting for the creels. For me it was a useful relaxation from studying, although the manilla was coarse on my soft fingers. The size of the creel coat depended on the size of the rectangular bottom, which varied in length between twenty-four inches and twenty-eight inches with a breadth of eighteen inches. Any rough day which confined us to the loft was spent in making creels. Father decided what the priorities were. The creel bottoms were usually hammered together, boring six holes with brace and bit for fitting the boughs. He preferred to fit the boughs himself, selecting three which appeared similar in a geometrical

Cellardyke fisherman John Clark hauling creels assisted by crew member George Sorley.
John Clark is a former Coxwain of the Anstruther Lifeboat.

Crail fisherman Harry Smith

sense. Three spars were placed along them, one on the top and one on either side to effect the rigidity of the creel. Undoubtedly the modern creels are much more shapely. We were both occupied in putting the netting on the creels. In April, after the winter herring fishing was over, we shot the creels for partans. They were on a messenger; that means a fleet of ten creels attached to a long rope, with a marker flag at each end, and you shot them anywhere as you would cross stretches of sand and rocks at random. Fresh bait was required each day for partans, as they ate the bait which had enticed them in. If you were unable to haul them for a day or two, the partans would make a hole in the netting after eating the bait.

Although my family gave me my chance to go to University, I was expected to go in the family yawls as an unpaid labourer. I always disliked going to the partan fishing, as you caught most when the water was thick with a north easterly swell, and the bait business was a serious problem. You couldn't go with as large a fleet of creels as you would wish, for lack of bait.

The skippers of the steam liners, however, were mindful of the creel men and they would bring home coal saithe on their home trips for bait. The steam drifters *Lasher* and *Pilot Star* were good to my father, who shared his supply with some of our other yawl men, who in turn gave us a share of any bait they got from their friends. The largest catch of partans I saw was over forty dozen (caught mainly off Caiplie Coves, the caves which lie between Cellardyke and Crail) in a motor yawl called the *Crest*, which my father had in partnership with James 'Patchie' Watson.

She was a good yawl, but the Atlantic paraffin engine gave so much trouble they were glad to sell her (at a good profit, by the way!). My father was later to fish out of Buckhaven with Patchie in the *Day Dawn* 168 DE, during several autumns, when the big boats were at Yarmouth. They caught a lot of lobsters, but had difficulty in getting a market for the partans as they were too dark. The redd from the Wellesley pit was blamed for that. The same redd ultimately completely ruined Buckhaven harbour.

In the 1920s and 30s we never got more than 1/6d per dozen for partans and 1/6d each for a lobster from Joe Smith and his father, Englishmen who had a shed near the head of the east pier. They used the four and a half inch gauge for the partans and the same one to measure the lobsters, from the point of its beak to the end of the carapace. If it was greater than four and a half inches, no matter how large it was, it was called a whole; slightly less it was called a half. This lasted for most of the 1930's until Burgon of Eyemouth sent a representative to buy by the pound; and great was father's delight when he sold a six-pounder for £1. I always enjoyed the lobster season. For one thing it started about the middle of July, and lobsters were not fastidious about the bait and obviously they did not go into the creel on scent, as half rotted mackerel covered with maggots from the blue fly caught as well as any fresh bait. Some years there were plenty of mackerel, and you caught enough of them to be salted down and kept for bait.

In some years, however, the mackerel were scarce and we would shoot a few taes of haddock lines in sandy holes to catch any kind of fish for bait. Black backed flounders were as good as anything. You always kept a few half soft partans, for which there was no market, to be used in emergency if you saw yourself running out of bait while hauling the creels.

One day when father was ill, I was out by myself and I baited the last creel to the west of the Hannah Harvey lighthouse on Anster West Pier with a soft partan. Sometimes you caught a lobster with that kind of bait, sometimes a codlin or large conger eel. This time I got two lemon soles, certainly the nearest to the harbour I had ever heard of them being caught.

Many strange stories are told about lobsters (I nearly said tall tales!). One year in the mid 1930s, we had our creels on Anster Easter Pier in the month of July preparing them for the lobster season. The position is important. They were leaning against the parapet wall, to the landward side of the place on the parapet where it changes from low to high as you go down the pier. If you look over the wall when the tide is out you will see the pools of water are about halfway between the high and low water marks. We were working at the creels when old David Corstorphine (former skipper of the steam drifter *Unity*) went down the pier accompanied by his grandson, Sonny, before coming back up again walking on the parapet. He said to my father: "I heard you lost a creel, there's a creel end floating over the back here". Sure enough, it was our colours of brown and green painted on the corks. Father said to me "You'll go down when the tide's out and I'll lower over a rope, and haul it up". I went down, accompanied by some boys who were our neighbours. There was the creel, partly out of the water, baited with a white piece of rubber from a sea boot and a shiny piece of tin, and in the creel were two lobsters. So, instead of hauling up the creel, father lowered some more over and we fished that area for the next fortnight with half a dozen creels. This let us see how far in the lobsters came to cast their shells, and that they went into the creels more on sight than anything else. So we tried many things for bait after that: broken white plates, white pieces of paper, herring guts in muslin bags, half rotten mackerel and all kinds of flounders. The Crail men, of course, working on a bigger scale, sent away for gurnets as they were firm and lasted for quite a while.

When we had the motor yawl *Families Pride,* we had been told of a good meads for hard ground off the Billowness. After shooting a fleet of 10 creels, father and I disagreed as to whether they had been shot properly, so he said. "Let's haul them again." So we did, and there were lobsters already in the creels, in a matter of minutes. I noticed the water looked dull, not completely thick, but greyish. I never forgot this, and we sometimes tried this successfully on seeing the water that colour.

Father had been dead now for some time, but I have a witness of another incident. David Smith of East Forth Street, Cellardyke, got me to take a share with him in a fourteen foot dinghy with outboard. We had about a dozen creels and tried the sproules for codlins and mackerels, but I came ashore when the school recommenced. As the season wore on he was considering taking the creels ashore, so I said I would help him. When I saw him on the Friday night, he said he'd got bait, and we went out and baited the creels and shot along the Ghat Skelly (the gateway to the harbour before the outer harbour was built). I said to him "I like the colour of the water, let's haul them again." So we started at the inner end. We got three lobsters. "Let's try it again." We got two. "That's enough," I said, but we had a youth with us who had been helping David. "Let's try it again," said he. We got one. "You'll be lucky if you get one, tomorrow." I said, as I could see the water beginning to clear, and one was what we got the following day.

I had better say something about the 'wulks,' or periwinkles, not whelks which are much larger. I will begin in a peculiar manner.

I have a copy of a beautiful book, *St. Andrews, City of Change* by Lamont Brown and Peter Adamson and on page eight, may be seen the picture of Sandy Chisholm who, as I have previously mentioned, was the last of the seven Chisholm brothers. 'Sandshoes' was his nickname and I was very friendly with him. We had bought and sold fishing gear with the Chisholm family for many years and knew the St. Andrews fishermen well. On looking up the Nautical Almanac for 1914, I saw the Chisholms had a boat, the *Wanderer*. The *Day Dawn* was owned by Peter Waters and the *George* by W. Hutchison, father of Jock Hutchison who won the Open Golf Championship in 1921. I wondered if I could connect the latter with the fishing in any way, so I asked 'Sandshoes' after seeing Jock Hutchison play in the Centenary Open. We saw him in the morning with a dark jersey on, while he played his one round on the Old Course for sentimental reasons and, in the afternoon, dressed with a soft hat, bow tie and Camel hair coat. In the forenoon like a St. Andrews fisherman and, in the afternoon, like a rich American!

When I asked 'Sandshoes' Chisholm if Hutchison had ever gone to the fishing, he said: "No, that I can mind, the Carnegies taen him awa to Americky when he left the schule, but I can mind gathering wulks wi' him and one o' my brithers doon ahent the Castle." So Jock Hutchison may have been the most distinguished wulk gatherer in the east of Fife, a number which includes many worthies.

I have been a wulk gatherer myself and I can make a few personal comments on gathering wulks. They were easiest gathered in cold weather as they clustered together, whereas in the summer they are scattered.

When I went to the wulks, there were so many people gathering them I doubt if I ever made more than 10/- in a week. We sold them to Joe Smith, the man who bought our partans. When you went into his shed, there was a pail standing on a piece of canvas that Joe called a cogue. It was the biggest pail I ever saw (some said it held two stone of wulks) and it had to be filled to overflowing, before we were rewarded with the sum of 1/6 per bucket. He swept up those wulks that had spilled over and kept them for himself.

102

Bob Latto hauling creels off St Monans

St Monans creel fisherman Bob Latto in his boat KY267 *Alert*

ML369 *Sunbeam* in Crail Harbour

Crail fisherman Robert Murray

I will close with a story about Joe Smith and his henchman, Eckie Birrell, his labourer, who pulled a two wheeled barrow down Anster East Pier for our meagre catches or to fill a barrel of water from the harbour to water the wulks in the shed to keep them alive, till they had a cargo for the goods station. I used to wonder at this latter behavior, as we were not allowed to gather wulks from inside the harbour, and we could see wulks galore climbing up the inner wall of the east pier during the summer. We were not allowed to gather them because, said Joe, they were contaminated by the oil and refuse which was discharged from the boats in the harbour. He added that he could see if anyone was taking them from inside the harbour from his shed at the head of the pier. But one day we were suspicious that somebody else was hauling our creels before us, so father said "we'll be up early the morn's morning". We shifted the yawl out to the end of the pier the previous night, as the tide could be out, got up between 3 a.m. and 4 a.m. and, as we went down the east pier, we heard voices. On looking over the pier, there were Joe and Eckie, gathering the wulks off the pier. We weren't allowed to gather them as they were reserved for supplying Joe with a rush order!

The local Fishery Office moved from Anster to Pittenweem about 1976-77, so the local returns in the statistics issued annually by the Scottish Office (Agriculture and Fisheries Dept.) were under Anster up to 1976 and thereafter under Pittenweem. I have therefore chosen a selection of local returns which were originally classified for prices as crabs per 100, then per dozen, then as metric tonnes and changed them as near as possible to price per stone for crabs, per lb. for lobsters, and per cwt for periwinkles (wulks) as this is how you will find Billingsgate prices reported at present in the Fishing News each week. Crabs proved the most difficult as they vary in size from 8 per stone to double that number, so you will find the price of crabs up to 1957 given per day while the price of periwinkles are only given from 1966. Before that they were only classed under 'other shellfish'.

Here is a cross section of prices, which I have adjusted where possible:

Year	Periwinkles	Crabs	Lobsters
1913		1/6 (7.5p) per dozen	1/1d (5.5p) each
1938		1/8˚d (8.5p) per dozen	1/4d (6.5p) each
1947		6/6d (32.5p) per dozen	3/10d (19p) each
1952		5/6d (27.5p) per dozen	3/10d (19p) each
1957		7/- (35p) per dozen	4/11d (24.5p) each
1958		6/9d (34p) per stone	4/3d (21.5p) per lb.
1963		7/- (35p) per stone	6/- (30p) per lb.
1966	39/8d (£1.98) per cwt.	7/- (35p) per stone	8/8d (43.5p) per lb.
1970	£2.50 per cwt.	43p per stone	58p per lb.
1975	£5.58 per cwt.	75p per stone	£1.42 per lb.
1980	£13.40 per cwt.	£1.46 per stone	£1.99 per lb.
1985	£18.65 per cwt.	£2.48 per stone	£3.27 per lb.
1990	£26.68 per cwt.	£4.68 per stone	
1991	£19.90 per cwt.	£4.49 per stone	£3.63 per lb.

Appendix I

Fishing Fleet Tables
for
Selected Ports
in the
East of Fife

St Andrews Boats in 1914:

Reg. No.	Vessel	Owners	Tons
DE 3	Families Pride	J. Brown.	20
DE 7	Symbol	T. Cunningham	7
DE 15	Children's Friend	Henry Brown.	10
DE 17	Vigilant	Peter Waters	36
DE23	Rover	John Waters	
DE30	Good Hope	David Gourlay	4
DE39	Nil Desperanda	J. & W. Cross	
DE44	Petunia	D. & A. Cunningham	3
DE45	Sally May	Jas. Brown	37
DE47	Toar	A. Harley Cunningham	3
DE49	Maggie	Robt. Wilson	5
DE53	Glade	J. & W. Cross	10
DE56	Wanderer	P. Chisholm	7
DE57	Nelson	A.J. and H. Gourlay	11
DE58	Alert	T. H. Smith	3
DE62	Queen	Owners unknown	3
DE64	George	W. Hutch ison	5
DE66	Sisters	R. Wilson & Son	3
DE57	Hearty	Henry Brown	4
DE176	Fisher Lassie	A. Gordon	
DE 74	Brothers	R. Cunningham	5
DE 76	Lizzie	J. Cargill	3
DE 79	Jessie	R. W. Cunningham	3
DE 86	Kate	Dr. A. Cunningham	1
DE103	Vine	J. Lister Jun.	12
DE152	Sisters	Jas. Brown.	5
DE161	Regent	T. P. Cunningham	6
DE164	Snowdrop	And. Gordon	6
DEl66	Agnes & Ellen	T. Black	4
DE167	Eagle	D. Melville & D. Stevenson	9
DE168	Day Dawn	P. Waters	9
DE169	Ann Noble	G. Brown	4
DEl70	Dominies Provider	J. Fenton	6
DE175	Catherine Black	Jas. Black	33
DE438	Livliehood	J. Lister Jun.	6
DE525	Jane & Lily	D. Gourlay	6
DE529	Highland Lassie	A. J. & H. Gourlay	9
DE579	Tappy	A. H. Gourlay	2

In 1914 the following St. Andrews boats were at the Drave:

Reg. No.	Vessel	Owners
DE22	Theodosia	J. & W. Cross
DE 3	Families Pride	J. Brown
DE 176	Fisher Lassie	A. Gordon
DE 175	Catherine Black	Jas. Black

Crail Boats in 1914:

Reg. No.	Vessel	Skipper	Tons
KY 85	Thistle	G. Boyter	2
KY 90	Jessie Bell	Jas. Meldrum	2
KY l08	Flower of Forest	D. Meldrum	3
KY 203	Good Samaritan	John Watson	3
KY 212	Guide Me	Jas. Watson.	3
KY 354	Elsie Edwards		2
KY 399	Families Pride	G. Grubb	4
KY 415	Jannette	J. & R. Cargill.	4
KY 432	Jessies	J Watson.	3
KY 452	Jessie's Jane	D. Black	2
KY 465	Jessie	Jas. Lorimer.	2
KY 470	Isabel	J. Jackson.	2
KY 476	Petrel	W. Gay	1
KY 490	Hope	A. Cunningham.	1
KY 510	Valkyrie	A. Cunningham.	2
KY 636	Vigilant	A. Cunningham.	2
ML 19	Lisitania	P. Cunningham	2
ML 35	Brothers	R. Dewar	3
ML 36	Sunbeam	R. Dewar	2
ML 81	Rippling Wave	A. Meldrum	2
ML 139	Annie Watson	J. Watson	2
ML 150	Mary Horsely	A. Sands	3
ML 156	Rose Craig	T. Meldrum	1
ML 179	Gazelle	W. Watson	1
ML 183	Sovereign II (Motor)	J. & R. Murray	6
ML 187	Ivy	G. Boyter	3
ML 210	Sydney Hill	A. Cogle	2
ML 214	Kia Ora	J. Watson	1
ML 270	Maggies	J. Peebles	5
ML 274	Barbara	R. Finlayson	1
ML 275	Be in Time	J. Watson	2
ML 293	Margaret	A. Cunningham	1

Anster and Cellardyke Fishing Fleet 1914, Kirkcaldy registered boats:

(SD denotes Steam Drifter)

Reg. No.	Vessel	Owners	Tons
KY 7	Nancy Dunn	A. & T. Thomson	48
KY21	Nil Desperandum	W. Murray & D.Carstairs	52
KY26	Snowflight	D. Lothian	36
KY36	Ebeneezer	James Muir	39
KY72	Refuge	S. Barclay	39
KY100	Camperdown (SD)	J. Muir & Others	
KY140	Plough (SD)	M. Gardner & Others	
KY151	Carmi	Thos. Anderson	35
KY162	Unity (SD)	D. Corstorphine & Others	
KY163	Primrose (SD)	R. Melville & Others	
KY165	Breadwinner	Henry Bett	39
KY183	Sisters	John Wilson	37
KY170	Morning Star (SD)	David Watson	37
KY176	East Neuk (SD)	Jas. Smith & Others	
KY178	Integrity (SD)	G. Anderson & Others	
KY179	White Rose	James Muir	
KY189	Evening Star (SD)	R. Hughes	
KY199	Venus (SD)	W. Smith & Others	
KY218	Pride o' Fife (SD)	John Watson	
KY220	Olive Leaf (SD)	W. Smith & Others	
KY245	Alices (SD)	John Jnr., Henry & W. Bett	27
KY251	Violet (SD)	W. Watson & Others	
KY255	Breadwinner (SD)	H. Bett	
KY276	Heidra (SD)	J. Smith & Others	
KY279	Craignoon (SD)	A. Rodger & Others	
KY285	Guerdon (SD)	Adam & Scott Beattie	
KY300	Carmi III (SD)		
KY301	Guide Me (SD)	R. Davidson	37
KY304	Kilmany (SD)	M. Gardner & Others	
KY313	Midlothian	W. & J. Watson	45
KY336	Shamrock	Jas. Pratt & Robt. Murray	33

Reg. No.	Vessel	Owners	Tons
KY373	Fruitful	John Deas	37
KY400	Lily	A. & J. Watson	49
KY407	Jeanie Woods	D. Wood (Birrell)	25
KY416	Jessie Hughes	D. Wilson	25
KY428	Gratitude	W. Watson	51
KY429	Weal	A. J. & D. Wood	20
KY436	Topaz	A. Gourlay	43
KY448	Ruby	J. D. & G. Wilson	51
KY458	Rab the Ranter (SD)	J. Brunton & Others	
KY469	Edith (SD)	P. Brown & A. Watson	
KY472	William Tennant (SD)	David Wood	
KY493	Glenogil (SD)	R. Stewart & Others	
KY571	White Cross (SD)	Alex Gourlay	
KY603	Vanguard III (SD)	M. Gardner & Others	
KY604	Invergellie (SD)	J. Muir	
KY618	Prima Donna	David Birrell	44
KY625	Families' Pride	T. Reid & T. Boyter 41	
KY630	Amethyst	Thos. Smith 37	
KY657	Henry Reid	D. Boyter & T. Reid	53
KY667	Jasper (motor)	A. Corstorphine	53
KY673	Betsy Smith	Brodie Smith	54

Anstruther and Cellardyke Fishing Fleet 1914, boats registered at Methil (mostly sailing boats):

Reg. No.	Vessel	Owners	Tons
ML2	Sceptre	David Davidson	55
ML16	Sunbeam (motor)	R. & D. Anderson	46
ML44	Mistletoe	P. Murray Jnr.	2
ML47	Harvest Home (motor)	T. Bett	44
ML57	Livelihood	John McRuvie	32
ML58	Onward	Robt. Anderson	1
ML95	John & Agnes	John Barclay	44
ML118	Prestige	J. Smith	52
ML136	Gem	R. Webster	37

111

Anstruther and Cellardyke Fishing Fleet 1914, boats registered at Methil (continued):

Reg. No.	Vessel	Owners	Tons
ML141	White Lily	A. Pratt & J. Moncrieff	39
ML145	Pansy	P. Smith	32
ML167	Lilias Scott	A. Gardner	47
ML168	Unity	John Dick	36
ML181	Fisher Lassie	R. Stuart & Others	15
ML192	Integrity	J. & A. Watson	43
ML198	Livelihope	J. Mair	41
ML203	Ocean's Gift	A. Ritchie	8
ML207	Unitas	A. Corstorphine	13
ML209	Stephanotis	J. Deas	11
ML213	Goldfinch	J. Watson	6
ML219	Welcome Home	A. McKay	8
ML220	Friendship	P. Muir	8
ML236	Water Lily	R. Watson	11
ML238	Andrews	J. Watson	6
ML266	Curlew	A. Marr	50
ML273	Rose	T. Muir	1
ML278	Betsy & Elizabeth	A. Keay	7
ML279	Glad Tidings	J. Watson & Others	15
ML282	Daisy	P. Melville	1
ML287	Maggies	R. Melville	1

Pittenweem Fishing Fleet 1914, boats registered at Kirkcaldy:

Reg. No.	Vessel	Owners	Tons
KY100	Preston Horsburgh	G Horsburgh	31
KY113	Storm King	Fergus Hughes	39
KY173	Nancy Hughes	Alex Hughes	33
KY195	Esther Watson	W. Hughes	5
KY225	Restless Ocean (Motor)	A. Hughes (Aitken)	37
KY229	Victoria Cross	G. Hughes (Butters)	37
KY233	Seiner	Dave Anderson	20
KY246	Celerity	W. Horsburgh & W. James	35
KY295	Lavinia	James Bowman	25
KY305	Fair Maid	D. Richards	20
KY384	Garland	R. Horsburgh	35
KY450	Never Can Tell	W. Wood (Hughes) & W. & J. Wood	27

Pittenweem Steam Drifters 1914, registered at Kirkcaldy:

Reg. No.	Vessel	Owners	Tons
KY121	Preston	George Horsburgh	84
KY134	Andrina	W. & A. Anderson	38
KY149	Restless Wave	R. Hughes Sen.	84
KY169	Azareal	William Lawson	95
KY188	Maggie Leask	W. Black & others	90
KY201	Tulip	Mitchell Hughes & others	88
KY217	Magdalen	John Hughes Montador	94
KY267	Calceolaria	Wm. Hutchison & Others	92
KY461	Anster Fair	T. Anderson	88

Pittenweem Fishing Fleet 1914, boats registered at Methil:

Reg. No.	Vessel	Owners	Tons
ML6	Useful	A. H. Aitken	5
ML17	Trustful	And. Anderson	1
ML24	Impregnable	George Flett	50
ML25	Fruitful Vine	John Simpson	40
ML46	Andrewina	A. Watson & W. & A. Anderson	51
ML55	Reliance	W. Hughes	37

Pittenweem Fishing Fleet 1914, boats registered at Methil (continued):

Reg. No.	Vessel	Owners	Tons
ML63	Try Again	Peter Anderson	51
ML68	Hope	And. Hughes	29
ML73	Merrimack	Jas. Robertson	35
ML74	Guide Me	Jas. Bowman	35
ML75	Violet (Motor)	R. Forbes	2
ML79	Christinia	W. Gay	56
ML82	Radiant	J. Horsburgh	42
ML85	Restless Waters	W. Bowman	43
ML106	Restless Wave	W. McBain	22
ML110	Thrive	R. Robertson	3
ML113	Annies	James Keay	3
ML131	Sunbeam	John Bowman	6
ML133	Lead On	A. Cameron	7
ML152	Choice	W. Watson	4
ML161	Alert	W. & A. Wood	5
ML175	Paraclete	J. Anderson	40
ML176	Maggies (Motor)	Andrew Watson	4
ML180	Sweet Promise	J. McKenzie	4
ML184	Snowdrop	J. G. McKenzie	4
ML194	Calceolaria	A. Wood	44
ML206	Majestic	And. Anderson	56
ML218	Golden Sunshine	R. Black	37
ML222	Wayside Flower	A. & T. Richards	49
ML226	Quiet Waters (Motor)	Jas. Hughes	6
ML230	Livelihope	Wm. Anderson	43
ML232	Daystar	Geo. Hughes	39
ML233	Laurel	Jas. Taylor	3
ML234	Christina Morrison	T. Mentiplay	6
ML235	Rising Sun (Motor)	Thos. Taylor	5
ML247	Hughes	T. & A. Hughes	46

Pittenweem Fishing Fleet 1914, boats registered at Methil (continued):

Reg. No.	Vessel	Owners	Tons
ML248	Regard	T. & A. Hughes	34
ML250	Ebenezer	John Smith	1
ML253	Fishers Friend	Robt. Gay	30
ML255	Safeguard (Motor)	Thos. Lawson	5
ML256	Branch	J., W. & A. Wood	49
ML257	Gays	Robt. Gay	3
ML259	Present Help (Motor)	Alex. Wood	5
ML260	United (Motor)	W. & A. Wood	4
ML262	Mascot (Motor)	Thos. Hughes	
ML263	Jamesina	W., D. & A. Black	9
ML277	Pride and Life	A. & A. Anderson	50
ML286	Margaret Lawson	T. Lawson	49
ML289	Pansy	John Watson	44
ML294	Bird	John Bowman	5
ML295	Daisy	A. & W. Anderson	2

St Monans Fishing Fleet 1914, boats registered at Kirkcaldy:

Reg. No.	Vessel	Owners	Tons
KY1	Mary Duncan (Motor)	David Duncan	40
KY16	Clan McKay	Robt. Jnr., T. & J. McKay	37
KY38	Elspeth Smith (Motor)	James Smith (Innes)	50
KY45	Hopeful	John Lowrie	30
KY51	Celtic	James McKay	40
KY67	Condor	D., J., R. & A. Smith	36
KY69	White Rose	W. Allan	42
KY81	Provider	John Easson	33
KY146	Chrysanthemum	A. Davidson & D. Irvine	40
KY156	Violet	Alex Hutt	41
KY213	Balmoral	J. Smith (Ogilvie)	39
KY280	Linaria Alba (Motor)	J. Innes (Scott)	40
KY286	Alice	Phillip Smith	40
KY293	Maggie Reekie	D. Reekie	39

St Monans Fishing Fleet 1914, boats registered at Kirkcaldy (continued):

Reg. No.	Vessel	Owners	Tons
KY303	Daisy	A. Meldrum	35
KY310	Helen Wilson	Wm. Wilson	40
KY395	Columbia	C. McKay	53
KY421	Gleaner	W. Marr	30
KY555	Isabella	Alex. Wood	33
KY556	Mackays	R. & D. Mackay	33
KY592	Busy Bee	J. A. Davidson	35
KY598	Ann Cook	P. & A. Fyall	37
KY599	Vigilant	James Adam	34
KY603	Nellie	J. Ovenstone (Allan)	31
KY615	Children's Trust	Wm. Reekie	36
KY639	Dayspring	Alex. Davidson	40
KY640	Vesper	R., W., D. & J. Smith	40
KY641	Watchful	A. & P. Aitken	35
KY646	Garland	J. Robertson & R. & W. Reekie	43
KY654	Vineyard	W. Mathers (Wood)	52
KY658	Fyalls	P., T., Alex. & And. Fyall	53
KY661	Sunshine	James Innes	54
KY664	Agnes Innes	Andrew Innes	54
KY665	Promote	R. Scott (Duncan) & others	52
KY666	Jessie Dunn	R. Dunn & Son	39

St Monans Fishing Fleet 1914, boats registered at Methil:

Reg. No.	Vessel	Owners	Tons
ML1	Lizzie Cameron	John Cameron	53
ML9	Pansy	Robt. Reekie	41
ML10	Glentanner	W. Sutherland	33
ML15	Harvest Moon	Wm. Gowans	40
ML20	True Vine	D. Marr	53
ML23	May Queen	Wm. Reekie	27
ML26	Glenyarrow	P. & J. Ovenstone	38
ML27	Majestic	D. & T. Aitken	36

116

St Monans Fishing Fleet 1914, boats registered at Methil (continued):

Reg. No.	Vessel	Owners	Tons
ML32	Thistle	R. Davidson	3
ML39	Prevail	Wm. Mathers	34
ML41	Marjory	Chas. Mackay	48
ML42	Nazzarullah	J. Anderson	35
ML48	Verbena	John Fernie, Jas. & R. Wilson	39
ML49	Falcon	Alex., Geo. & Robt. Allan	56
ML50	Agnes Irvine	Alex Irvine	52
ML60	Nightingale	Wm., John, Robt. & Alex Dunn	41
ML61	Ocean's Gift	J. Gowans	51
ML71	Rejoice	Alex. Davidson	48
ML72	Emblem	D. & R. Smith	54
ML78	Jeannie	John Fyall	10
ML84	Chrysoprase	David Morris	40
ML87	Vineyard	Jas. Gowans	44
ML89	Scotch Thistle	Alex. Meldrum & Chas. Smith	45
ML90	Campanulia	W. Marr & W. Gay	35
ML91	Maggies	D. Ovenstone & John Gay	40
ML93	Honey Bee	David Allan	47
ML94	Beautiful Star	David Smith	30
ML96	Young Dan	R. Robertson & T. Guthrie	37
ML97	Trust On	Chapman Lowrie	40
ML99	Reform	John Fyall	42
ML103	Research	John Hutt	43
ML116	Olive	Peter Dunn	14
ML117	White Heather	A. Morris	43
ML120	Diligent	James Miller	12
ML121	Better Luck	A. Hutt	11
ML129	Children's Friend	A. Scott & others	43
ML131	Boy James	W. & T. Tarvet	42
ML132	Ebeneezer	Geo. Davidson	41
ML140	Johan	John Allan	49
ML146	Elizabeth Young	David Young	47
ML155	Lily of the Valley	G. & A. Gerrard	38

St Monans Fishing Fleet 1914, boats registered at Methil (continued):

Reg. No.	Vessel	Owners	Tons
ML158	Hope	Peter Gerrard	38
ML159	Grateful	J., D. & T. Gay	39
ML160	Davidson	W. & R. Davidson	13
ML163	Dayspring	J. Hutt & C. Innes	9
ML171	Daisy	James Reekie	
ML172	Auricula	John Gillies	64
ML182	Standard	J. Hutt	4
ML190	Barbara Davidson	R. Wood	40
ML193	Jessie	J. Ovenstone	49
ML197	Seagull	P. Hughes	
ML199	Alert	P. Ovenstone	43
ML201	Coronilla	R. Hutt	35
ML205	Barbara Wood	W. Wood	37
ML217	Renown		40
ML221	Glencona	T. & W. Hutt	10
ML223	Sceptre	John Mayes	11
ML225	Enterprise	P. & R. Aitken	9
ML227	Fragrance	W. Guthrie	41
ML228	Village Maid	P. Scott & J. Mair	40
ML237	Chrysolite	A. Reekie	40
ML239	Guiding Star	Wm. Mathers	14
ML240	Spero Meloria (motor)	A. Irvine	11
ML241	Celerity	And. Smith	42
ML242	True Vine	James Innes	42
ML243	Star of Hope	John Mayes	45
ML244	Cheerful	Wm. Allan	40
ML245	Carmania	R., W. & J. Smith	44
ML251	Jessie Mathers	W. Mathers	5
ML260	Kate	John Davidson	4
ML261	Frigate Bird (motor)	Wm. Wilson	10
ML264	M.R.A.	Alex. Aitken	15
ML265	Hesperus	John Lowrie	14

St Monans Fishing Fleet 1914, boats registered at Methil (continued):

Reg. No.	Vessel	Owners	Tons
ML267	Good Design	T. Mathers & T. Guthrie	44
ML268	Mayflower		45
ML269	Golden Queen	James Allan	39
ML271	Celandine	And. Innes	45
ML280	Protect Me	Robt. Marr	47
ML281	Mizpah	Alex. Wood	15
ML283	Buttercup	Jas. Guthrie	2
ML284	Beryl	David Hutt	44
ML285	Annie Mathers	Chapman Mathers	48
ML288	Ocean Reward	D., D. & G. Lowrie	44
ML290	Vine	A. Balfour	49
ML291	Hazel	James Allan	50
ML292	Primula	Geo. Robertson	53

St Monans Steam Drifters in 1914:

Reg. No.	Vessel	Owners	Tons
ML122	Lizzie Hutt	Jas. Hutt, C. Innes & Eliza Hutt	82
ML123	Christina Mayes	John Mayes	82
ML125	Mackays	Robt., Thos. & Jas. Mackay	83
ML126	Janet Reekie	W., R., D., A. & C. Reekie	81
ML164	Diligence	T. & A. Adam	85
KY143	Camelia	A., P., & R. Aitken	85
KY152	Pursuit	J. Wood	79
KY172	Lucy Mackay	R., W. & J. McKay & P. Marr	94

Elie & Earlsferry Boats in 1914

Reg. No.	Vessel	Owners	Tons
KY 231	Maud	D. Thomson	20
KY 552	Active	A. Thomson	18
KY 1719	Janet	James Webster	27

Largo Boats in 1914:

Reg. No.	Vessel	Owners	Tons
KY 34	Brothers	John Clunie	2
KY 289	Violet	David Gillies	$^1/_2$
KY 307	Rose	James Melville	1
KY 435	Isabella Dutch	D. Melville	5
KY 455	Eva Anstruther	T. Lawrie	5
KY 463	Kate	D. Ballingall	3
KY 468	Thistle	A. Simpson	1
KY 523	Osprey	W. Gillies	2
KY 533	Brothers	D. Ballingall	2
KY 675	Lily	D. Gillies	1
KY 681	Emerald	J. Bell	
ML 14	Lively	D. Ballingall	3
ML 21	Unity (20, 22)	T. Wishart, D & J Melville.	2
ML 208	Venture (20, 22, 30, 32, 38, 39)	W Hutton	3
ML 254	Crusoe (20, 22, 26, 28, 30)	J. W. & J. Gillies	3
ML 46	Clarewood (38)	J. & D. Lawrie & D. Melville	3.4
ML 64	Brenda (38)	W. Hutton & J. Clunie	1.11
ML 86	Azriel (39)	D. Melville	1.29

(The numbers in brackets signify the date of the Almanac in which the boat's name appears).

120

Buckhaven Boats in 1914:

Reg. No.	Vessel	Owners	Tons
KY20	Delight	T. Robertson	4
KY136	Agnes & Mary	D. Taylor	2
KY223	Betsy	Wm. Walker	43
KY355	Jessie	Jas. Easson	5
KY438	Ocean Foam	Robt. Walker	3
KY505	Gratti the Leader	John Deas (Emma)	25?
KY506	Empress	W., John & Jas. Thomson	23
KY685	Maggie & Annie	Wm. Walker	
ML3	Sisters	John Deas	2
ML8	Isa	James Glover	2
ML22	Katie & Mary	Peter Thomson	3
ML43	Momentus	J. Easson	63
ML53	Agenora	R. Thomson	1
ML54	Fisher Lass	W. Easson	52
ML59	Maggie	A. Taylor	1
ML77	Pioneer	Jas. Robertson	5
ML98	Eureka	Jas. Robertson	4
ML100	Guide	Jas. Robertson	1
ML115	Isabella		33
ML138	Glengarry	R. & W. Walker	35
ML142	Maggie Scott	J. & R. Walker	25
ML143	Osprey		1
ML147	Cecilia	And. Walton	1
ML148	Brothers	Jas. Taylor	1
ML165	Mayflower	T. Bell & A. Walker	1
ML174	Thistle	W. Thomson	3
ML185	Heather Bell	John Thomson	2
ML200	Caroline	J. Logie	2
ML204	Lizzie	G. Gordon	1
ML215	Amiable	Jas. Taylor	6
ML216	Gipsy Maid	W. Robertson	2
ML224	Comfort	Jas. Thomson	1
ML249	Paragon	John Warrender	1
ML258	Maggie	J. Deas	3
ML276	Pearl	J. Deas	2

121

1918: List of **Buckhaven** boats **with** **fishing permits:**

Reg. No.	Vessel	Owners
ML320	Alice	R. Thomson, Bernard Court.
ML 18	Industry (26)	Jas. Thomson, 3 Deas Square.
ML 22	Katie & Mary (26)	Peter Thomson, 4 East Shore Street.
ML 316	Britannia	W. Robertson, Randolph Street.
ML 345	Lark	T. Thomson, 5 Cargill Road.
ML 309	Expedient	Jas. Taylor, 2 Bethune Square.
ML 187	Ivy (26)	Henry Taylor (Sen.), 20 Cargill Road.
ML 249	Paragon	Alan Foster, 177 Randolph Street.
ML 108	Guide	T. Robertson, 11 Ireland Square.
ML 53	Agenora (26, 30)	R. Thomson, 3 W. Shore Street.
ML 318	Boy Bob (26, 30)	G. Thomson, John Bones.
ML 434	Glasgow Lassie	Jas. Deas, Mitchell Street.
ML 359	Maggie Deas (26, 40)	John Deas, 3 Bonthron Lane.
ML 396	Flora	John Glover, 12 Cairns Square.
ML 360	Comely (26, 30)	Andrew Deas, 150 W. High Street.
ML 319	Jenny (26, 30)	Jas. Taylor (Kinnear) 35 E. High St.
ML 200	Caroline (26)	And. Taylor, 111 Goodmans Bldgs.
ML 147	Cecilia	And. Watson, 44 W. High Street.
ML 347	Poppy	Jas. Robertson, 30 Randolph Street.
ML 314	Allies	T. Taylor, 38 W. High Street
ML 470	Active (26)	Jas. Thomson, 15 East Shore Street.
ML 258	Maggie	Jas. Glover, 172 West High Street.
ML 446	Venus	W. Logie, 122 Randolph Street
ML 439	Meg	R. T. Foster, 18 Mitchell Street.
ML 339	Minnie (26)	Jas. Warrender, W. High Street.

(The figures in brackets which appear after certain boats' names indicate that
these boats are also listed in 1926, 1930 or 1940)

Pittenweem Fishing Fleet 1937

Number	Name	Owner	Length	Age
ML51	True Love	Anderson	71ft	30 years
ML 257	Canny Scot	Bowman	23ft	30 years
ML 180	Sweet Promise	McKenzie	27ft	26 years
ML 260	United	Wood	26ft	26 years
ML 8	Jessie	Hughes	30ft	25 years
ML 161	Alert	Bowman	27ft	25 years
ML 176	Maggies	Watson	27ft	25 years
ML 226	Quiet Waters	Galloway	27ft	25 years
ML 81	Rippling Wave	Boyter	22ft	23 years
ML 48	Helpmate	Bowman	37ft	20 years
ML 65	Blossom	Bowman	30ft	20 years
ML 150	Boy Andrew	Mentiplay	22ft	20 years
ML 166	Ivy Leaf	Hughes	32ft	20 years
KY 64	Seton Castle	Hughes & McBain	27ft	20 years
KY 294	Bird	Mackay	28ft	19 years
KY 455	Launch Out	Wood	32ft	18 years
ML 10	Briar	Bowman	33ft	15 years
KY 144	Fortunate	Hughes	45ft	15 years
KY 112	Olive	Hughes	32ft	15 years
ML 105	Volunteer	Wood	30ft	14 years
ML 21	Glint	Hughes	43ft	12 years
ML 55	Trusty	Horsburgh	33ft	12 years
KY 135	Courageous	Wilson	33ft	12 years
KY 246	Rejoice	Wood	32ft	9 years
KY 193	Bright Ray	Anderson	47ft	8 years
KY 41	Golden Chance	Bowman	32ft	6 years
KY 47	Boy Alex	Bowman	33ft	6 years
KY 49	Eulogia	Lindsay	36ft	5 years
KY 100	Enterprise	A. Mackay	36ft	5 years
ML 39	Sparkling Waters	Hughes	36ft	3 years
KY 15	Amber Queen	Watson	45ft	2 years
KY 59	Courageous II	Wilson	47ft	1 year
KY 56	Emulate	Hughes	56ft	$1/_2$ year
KY 51	Argosy	Lawson	53ft	$1/_2$ year
KY 110	Floral Queen	Watson	47ft	$1/_4$ year
KY 115	Good Design	Watson	47ft	$1/_4$ year

St Monans Motor and Sailing Boats in 1939:

Reg. No.	Vessel	Owners	Tons
KY102	Kimberley	T. A. Adam & J. Adam	102
KY145	Godetia	T. Gowans	17
KY156	Protect Us	W.Tarvit & J. Ovenstone	17
KY171	Celtic	P Marr, R Marr & J. Marr	19
KY172	Lucy Mackay	W.Mackay & W. Meldrum.	94
KY173	White Heather II	TGay	25
KY181	Procyon	W Allan R Smith	29.76
KY184	Flush	M. Gowans	97
KY197	Scarlet Thread	T.Adam, E.Adam & A.Adam	96.45
KY208	Defensor	R. Marr.	84
KY245	Clan Mackay	R Mackay	47

St Monans Sailing and Motor Boats:

Reg. No.	Vessel	Owners	Tons
KY7	Spanish Castle	A. R. Cameron & M.D. Cameron	26
KY18	Mizpah	John Cameron	12
KY38	Elspeth Smith	J. & A. T. Smith	53.37
KY39	Diligence	P. Gerrard	17.05
KY54	Paragon	A. & D. Hutt	15
KY66	Carmonia II	J.(sen.) & J.(jun.) Smith & G. Mair	36.65
KY133	Nancy	D. Gowans	2
KY134	Girl Christian	T. Gerrard	29.48
KY114	Village Maid	D. Fleming	1
KY118	Tern	Jas. Miller	0.87
ML1	Lilac	John Wilson	1.76
ML15	Harvest Moon	A. & J. Gowans	39.69
ML38	Gowan	S. Smith and W. Mackie	39.44
ML41	Marjory	G. Mackay	47.60
ML52	Perseverance	J. Mayes & W. Thomson	12.15
ML80	Endeavour	J. D. & R. Cargill	40.22
ML150	Boy Andrew	T. & A. Mentiplay	2.81
ML198	Lively Hope	J. Allan ju n	41.00
ML240	Faithful	W.Mayes. A. Anderson & A. Irvine	16.51
ML241	Celerity	J. Mayes & J. Smith	42.00
ML271	Celandine	A. Innes	45.37
ML285	Annie Mathers	C.J. & W. Mathers	48.22
ML487	Condor	J. Lowrie & A. Smith.	47.12

Crail Fisherman Harry Smith shows off a sizeable lobster

Alf Smith on board his creel boat KY207 *Betty Smith*

Robert Murray and son at Crail Harbour

Appendix II
East Fife Fishing Fleet Statistics Tables

1928 to 1948

St Andrews Fishing Industry Statistics from 1928 to 1948

Year	Motor Boats Over 30ft	Motor Boats Under 30ft	Sailing Boats Under 30ft	Total Tonnage	No. of Men Employed	Whitefish Landed (Cwt)	Value of Whitefish Landed (£)	Value of Shellfish Landed (£)
1928	4	1	11	56	30	1,314	1,042	3
1932	0	9	6	40	16	857	615	91
1933	0	8	5	35	17	72	94	73
1934	0	8	5	35	18	63	88	111
1935	0	9	5	40	17	52	75	56
1936	0	9	5	40	18	38	54	35
1937	0	9	5	40	18	53	72	18
1938	0	6	3	30	18	46	61	22
1939	0	5	2	21	16	50	63	135
1940	0	4	2	18	12	69	129	139
1942	0	9	3	31	14	47	146	266
1943	0	11	3	32	14	33	109	533
1944	0	10	3	24	10	22	63	588
1945	0	13	1	26	11	30	79	527
1946	0	15	1	28	12	27	77	613
1948	0	12	0	25	16	27	51	524

Crail Fishing Industry Statistics from 1928 to 1946

Year	Motor Boats	Sailing Boats	Total Tonnage	No. of Men Employed	Whitefish Landed (Cwt)	Value of Whitefish Landed (£)	Value of Shellfish Landed (£)
1928	9	10	55	47	749	659	4,454
1932	8	10	44	32	441	368	3,114
1933	8	8	44	38	235	204	3,546
1934	9	10	48	41	112	87	3,264
1935	11	8	49	35	249	176	2,447
1936	11	8	49	36	227	171	2,690
1937	12	6	48	39	336	252	2,593
1938	12	6	48	39	65	48	2,878
1939	12	3	40	34	0	0	2,508
1940	14	3	42	20	344	481	2,993
1942	13	5	44	23	28	65	8,803
1943	16	4	50	23	0	0	11,373
1944	16	4	50	23	0	0	11,459
1945	18	3	51	30	5	10	14,405
1946	20	3	58	51	85	155	21,115

Anster and Cellardyke Fishing Industry Statistics from 1928 to 1948

Year	Steam Drifters	Motor Boats Over 30ft	Motor Boats Under 30ft	*Sailing Boats	Total Tonnage	No. of Men Employed	Whitefish Landed (Cwt)	Value of Whitefish Landed (£)	Value of Shellfish Landed (£)
1928	35	9	5	14	1528	405	803	782	1,170
1932	32	7	4	10	1424	378	765	629	669
1933	29	7	3	8	1372	351	583	463	731
1934	29	6	1	9	1300	342	421	345	785
1935	26	5	1	6	1178	314	531	388	889
1936	25	5	1	7	1139	300	324	265	725
1937	21	7	1	8	1064	274	273	207	785
1938	**19	7	1	6	992	252	389	275	836
1939	16	10	2	4	939	226	410	273	401
1940	0	1	4	4		29	398	633	338
1942	0	2	6	6	60	34	3,220	8,627	646
1943	0	3	4	5	70	34	16,885	42,878	989
1944	0	4	5	5	97	55	15,435	41,319	966
1945	0	7	5	4	177	66			
1946	3	9	3	3	531	126	17,315	36,168	1,385
1948	3	10	6	0	441	131	5,642	12,823	1,106

*All sailing boats were under 30ft in length
**In 1938, two of the steam drifters were fitted with transmitting apparatus

Pittenweem Fishing Industry Statistics from 1928 to 1948

Year	Steam Drifters	Motor Boats Over 30ft	Motor Boats Under 30ft	*Sailing Boats	Total Tonnage	No. of Men Employed	Whitefish Landed (Cwt)	Value of Whitefish Landed (£)	Value of Shellfish Landed (£)
1928	6	9	21	5	638	219	12,533	14,820	
1932	4	7	28	3	554	182	11,995	12,634	13
1933	3	13	24	3	545	173	13,388	13,973	
1934	3	14	22	3	553	176	11,316	11,763	
1935	2	16	20	3	477	167	11,914	12,009	
1936	1	20	20	3	536	176	11,810	11,964	
1937	0	19	18	1	438	162	12,649	13,284	
1938	0	19	17	1		245	10,117		
1939	0	17	16	1	409	146	12,443	14,951	
1940	0	10	20	1	216		13,895	31,177	338
1942	0	13	16	1	237	110	12,475	31,412	41
1943	0	15	13	1	251	110	11,383	28,003	91
1944	0	16	8	1	234	110	9,565	24,176	163
1945	0	15	6	1	224	114	7,961	18,210	130
1946	0	16	7	1	268	121	15,826	32,049	134
1948	0	18	11	0	390	157	9,173	21,276	469

* All sailing boats under 30ft

131

St Monans Fishing Industry Statistics from 1928 to 1948

Year	Steam Drifters	Motor Boats Over 30ft	Motor Boats Under 30ft	Sailing Boats	Total Tonnage	No. of Men Employed	Whitefish Landed (Cwt)	Value of Whitefish Landed (£)	Value of Shellfish Landed (£)
1928	11	44	4	6	1,576	436	3,545	5,197	84
1932	7	35	4	3	1,500	304	767	1,026	41
1933	6	35	3	3	1,487	291	1,206	1,389	75
1934	6	35	2	3	1,476	285	1,979	2,749	84
1935	5	35	1	2	1,328	283	3,545	5,197	84
1936	5	34	1	2	1,328	283	2,315	3,439	
1937	3	34	2	1	1,263	283	2,094	3,430	
1938	4	33			1,216	276	2,977	4,623	
1939	3	31	4	1	1,130	245	2,402	3,265	37
1940		15	3	1	439	122	1,250	3,603	3
1942		12	5	2	239	113	7,662	18,350	49
1943		8	6	2	177	113	11,093	26,555	89
1944		7	6	2	161	117	9,914	22,969	166
1945		10	2	2	409	105	12,586	26,884	102
1946		14	5	2		92	19,294	37,726	144
1948		10	5	2	242	92	4,454	9,047	254

As you might notice, 1947 is omitted from the above table. This was the year when there was the worst winter weather I ever experienced, when the country was afflicted by the Siberian anticyclone. The 'sky in the sea mouth', as my father called it, was of a greenish colour for about six weeks and one blizzard followed another

Elie & Earlsferry Fishing Industry Statistics from 1928 to 1948

Year	Motor Boats	Sailing Boats	Total Tonnage	No. of Men Employed	Whitefish Landed (Cwt)	Value of Whitefish Landed (£)	Value of Shellfish Landed (£)
1928		3	3	6	85	121	
1932		2	2	4	93	126	
1933		2	2	4	68	91	
1934		2	2	4	44	51	
1935		2	2	4	23	28	16
1936		2	2	4	35	43	28
1937		2	2	4	73	75	33
1938	1	1	3	4	47	34	54
1939	1	1	1	2	59	69	26
1940	2	1	3	4	44	80	12
1942		1	1	2			
1943		1	1	2	7	21	26
1944		1	1	2	10	40	19
1945	1	1	2	3	18	20	
1946	1	1	2	2			
1948	1	1		2			

Largo Fishing Industry Statistics from 1928 to 1948

Year	Motor Boats	Sailing Boats	Total Tonnage	No. of Men Employed	Whitefish Landed (Cwt)	Value of Whitefish Landed (£)	Value of Shellfish Landed (£)
1928	3	7	18	31	1,348	1,698	
1932	4	5	15	20	1,114	1,367	
1933	3	4	12	15	649	717	
1935	4	3	13	14	485	516	
1936	4	3	13	14	503	364	
1937	5	2	14	14	257	190	
1938	3	2	8	14	234	190	
1939	3	3	8	14	287	276	
1940	2	5	9	14	241	480	
1942	2	5	8	11	157	399	
1943	2	5	9	11	42	130	102
1944	2	5	9	8	33	111	102
1945	2	5	9	8	44	135	
1946	3	1	9	7	85	162	80
1948	3	1	9	7	3	4	63

Methil Fishing Industry Statistics from 1928 to 1948

Year	Motor Boats	Sailing Boats	Total Tonnage	No. of Men Employed	Whitefish Landed (Cwt)	Value of Whitefish Landed (£)	Value of Shellfish Landed (£)
1928		3	3	6	84	114	13
1932		4	6	8	119	182	16
1933		4	6	8	109	141	16
1934		4	6	8	82	82	
1935		2	3	4	33	35	
1936	1	2	4	8	159	130	4
1937		2	3	4	154	180	15
1938		2	3	4	180	242	3
1939	12	4	25	24	224	397	11
1940	21	4	39	16	211	463	15
1942	26	16	57	19	450	1,259	70
1943	30	18	61	19	275	858	93
1944	30	16	66	20	355	945	152
1945	26	16	56	20	561	1,518	38
1946	34	11	73	27	787	1,700	82
1948	41	10	85	31	882	2,017	119

Buckhaven Fishing Industry Statistics from 1928 to 1948

Year	Motor Boats	Sailing Boats	Total Tonnage	No. of Men Employed	Whitefish Landed (Cwt)	Value of Whitefish Landed (£)	Value of Shellfish Landed (£)
1928	5	12	37	28	1,507	2,341	14
1932	4	6	25	20	1,115	1,441	56
1933	4	6	25	20	710	938	45
1934	4	6	25	20	254	323	61
1935	4	3	19	16	372	480	69
1936	4	3	19	16	365	44	
1937	4	2	17	14	22	48	
1939	3		11	9	45	55	
1940	3		11	7	30	65	
1942	3		7	6	20	45	10
1943	3		7	6	14	45	
1944	6	2	18	8		116	40
1945	5	2	15	8	39	95	
1946	1		37	13	50	82	42
1948	1	5		6	No Returns. Landings at Methil or Wemyss.		

Auctioneer W.Hughes at Pittenweem fish market

KY995 *Crusader* about to land her catch of prawns at Pittenweem

Boxes of prawns about to be landed at Pittenweem market

Appendix III

Fish Landings

at

Pittenweem

in

Metric Tonnes

1950-1999

1950s

Year	Demersal	Pelagic	Shellfish	Total
1950	896	0	0	896
1951	752	2	0	752
1952	968	1	0	969
1953	1236	0	0	1236
1954	1501	6	0	1507
1955	1370	5	0	1375
1956	1525	18	0	1543
1957	1414	15	0	1429
1958	1192	51	195	1438
1959	1415	50	297	1762

1960s

Year	Demersal	Pelagic	Shellfish	Total
1960	1686	164	161	2011
1961	1776	211	163	2150
1962	2168	130	222	2520
1963	2067	247	211	2525
1964	3020	52	166	3238
1965	2792	91	239	3122
1966	2171	16	454	2641
1967	2463	8	202	2673
1968	454	1	61	516
1969	3790	1014	400	5204

1970s

Year	Demersal	Pelagic	Shellfish	Total
1970	3770	17	623	4410
1971	3885	399	513	4797
1972	4245	132	682	5059
1973	4909	10	678	5597
1974	3878	129	592	4599
1975	3681	6	578	4265
1976	4003	43	744	4790
1977	3212	2	704	3918
1978	4171	1	550	4722
1979	4570	2	453	5025

1980s

Year	Demersal	Pelagic	Shellfish	Total
1980	4907	7	430	5344
1981	5107	3	467	5577
1982	4148	2	560	4710
1983	3565	1	724	4290
1984	3491	0	785	4276
1985	3303	1	1014	4318
1986	2658	27	1263	3948
1987	2674	67	704	3445
1988	1515	15	1166	2696
1989	1037	7	849	1893

1990s

Year	Demersal	Pelagic	Shellfish	Total
1990	847	5	940	1792
1991	1103	9	753	1865
1992	1313	10	959	2282
1993	1576	17	1143	2736
1994	864	3	844	1711
1995	1315	1	1144	2460
1996	1402	4	1002	2408
1997	1249	1	1287	2537
1998	1003	1	1302	2306
1999	435	0	1300	1735

Appendix IV: Totals of Registered Fife Fishing Boats in 1999

Creek	Vessels of 10 Metres and Over	Vessels Under 10 Metres
Anstruther	12	18
Burntisland	0	2
Crail	0	8
Methil and Leven	4	10
Pittenweem	14	12
St Andrews	0	17
St Monans	2	6
Total	**32**	**73**

142

Landing prawns at Pittenweem

Inside the fish market at Pittenweem

Appendix V: An Undated Early View of Anster Shore Street

There are many points of interest in this photograph.

(1) The former Post Office is not completely built. George Doig, a former counter employee there, said he heard the building dated from 1878.

(2) I once wrote an article about the building of the East Pier, so I looked it up. Construction was started in 1866 and the pier took ten years to build. The *East Fife Record* on 15 December 1876 states that: "The old harbour mouth is closed with a temporary bridge over it before the roadway is made". The photograph clearly shows several people standing inside the harbour, which would indicate that the harbour bottom consisted mainly of sand and not mud. This would mean that the old harbour mouth was still open, which would date the photograph at 1877 plus or minus one year.

(3) There was an accident at the harbour which occurred when concrete slabs were being laid at the back of the new East Pier. The blocks were

made some time before they were required and left in the harbour to season. Two large floating tubs or punts were used to float them round, one of which can be seen in the picture. The blocks were between 12 and 14 tons in weight and a thick piece of wood was placed between the punts, from which blocks were suspended by ropes. The cutting of the ropes at one and the same moment was not done and this upset one of the punts containing John Linn and James Waterston. Both were rescued by the towing boat. I heard this story long before I read it and when anything in the harbour required simultaneous action or when a glass was being filled with some beverage, someone would be sure to say, "Say when, John Linn".

(4) To the east of the punt and fishing boat may be seen a pile of wood, and I will now quote from Gourlay's book *Anstruther*: "There were as many as five vessels on the stocks at one time and it seems that the part of the 'Folly' at the west end was land reclaimed from the sea, therefore doing away with the 'spending beach'. This led to the erection of the 'Woodyard' or 'The Folly', for as the skipper cursed the Bailies between his teeth, he held to the stem rope with his vessel rolling and twisting like a wild bull in the range of the sea."

(5) The fishing boats appear to have been tarred and there is no appearance of a white 'mouthpiece' on the bow, a thing which was never mentioned by Auld Wull. In the only photo we have of the boats lying, laid up in the Town's Green, however, the mouthpiece is very much in evidence (see photograph on page 25).

(6) The only two boat builders mentioned about this time are Millar and Jarvis, who later built most of the Steam Liners. As these boats were built mainly at the east end of Shore Street, Millar appears to be the boat builder seen in this view.

Anstruther harbour packed with ring net boats from the Clyde. *Betty II* is nearest to the camera and alongside her are BA177 *Morea* and BA252 *Aurora II*. Note the fish boxes piled high on 'The Folly' in the background.

Line boats storm bound at Pittenweem

Appendix VI: A Day at the Sma' Line Fishing

A Personal Account by Andrew Watson

The alarm clock goes at 4 a.m. After having a cup of tea, it is jacket on, piece box tucked under oxter and down to the boat for 4.30 a.m. The first crewman on board puts on the galley fire. Some paper sticks and coal doused with diesel oil ignited by a match soon has the cabin beginning to warm up. As we are going out with ebbing water and there are still a few hours until daylight appears, we cruise at half speed towards the May Island.

With daylight breaking in the sky we prepare to shoot the lines - two per crewman, each line having 600 hooks all baited with mussel. A scull is placed on the boxes and beside a man sitting on the after side of the wheel house, on the weather side with a roller in his hand. Away goes the dahn. The dahn is tied to a length of rope to which a stone weight is tied at a length which enables the dahn to float freely on top of the water with the stone lying on the seabed. From the stone another few fathoms of rope which is tied to the first line makes sure that the lines will be at the bottom. The line starts to run out over the roller. The roller guides the line and keeps it from being blown on board the boat. The individual lines are knotted together and as a scull empties it is quickly pulled away and replaced by a full one. When all the sculls are empty there would be a stone, rope and dahn as on the other end. We would lie at one end of the dahn, depending on the direction of the wind and tide for one to one and a half hours.

A welcome pot of tea is brewed and the piece box opened and a general talk among the crew takes place.

Then comes a call from the skipper. Time to start hauling. On board comes the dahn, followed by rope and line. An empty scull is placed mid-ships on boxes, and a crewman starts to haul the line on the fore side of the scull. A second man sits behind the scull and a third man sits on the after side of the scull. As well as helping the second man to take the fish off the hooks and clean the hooks of bait and starfish, this third man is responsible for the scum net. This net is used to scoop fish on board that are too heavy to be lifted on board by hand, or any fish that fall back into the sea from broken hooks or any other reason. After the first line is hauled, the crewmen rotate their positions, so that all have a turn to haul and to sit, until all the lines are hauled. Then we are underway for the harbour but first a mug of tea with what was left in the piece box. This done, all the crew go on deck and start gutting the fish and putting them into different boxes according to size and species, whilst trying all the while to keep their balance as best they can, as the boat is now usually punching into a fresh wind.

On arriving in harbour, the fish are landed on an open fish market, then covered by a tarpaulin to keep the gulls away. The sculls are hauled onto the pier, the boat is moored and then it is home for a warm meal.

After the meal the sculls are wheel barrowed to the house or out shed (in good weather this was done outside) where the lines are cleaned of all old bait and starfish and then the redd into the scull, and repaired as needed as there could be broken hooks, stranded hemp or snaids needing renewed. When this is all done, the lines are left to be baited next day by the womenfolk, who had spent the morning when we were at sea baiting another set of lines and these were taken to the boat and put on board ready for the next morning.

By this time it was 4 to 5 p.m. if you were lucky.

The rest of the day, or often just evening, is our own until it is time to start again. Where we will fish tomorrow depends on what was caught today and also on weather conditions.

Appendix VII: The *Sedulous*

A Personal Account by Skipper William McBain
(Taken from a tape recording)

At the start of the sixties I was Skipper of the *Sedulous*, which I had built in 1965 at Millers in St. Monans. She was 49.9 ft. with a beam of 16'9 - this was so we were allowed to work in the Firth if it was bad weather, where the boats had to be below 50 ft. In the winter time we worked mainly anywhere in the Firth to out as far as the Wee Bankie and the Cockenzie Bank. The Wee Bankie was about 25 miles east by south east of the May Island and Cockenzie Bank was just a wee bit to the North East of that.

Our holiday was a fortnight in the summer time, when we got our overhaul, Christmas Day and a day or two at the new year. We were mainly catching whitings, codlins and haddocks in the winter time and just an odd flat fish. In the summer time we worked from the Wee Bankie as far out as 100 miles, but when it came to the months of August, September and into October we used to work the flat fish about 48 - 50 miles east and by north from the May Island. Very occasionally we went to the prawns and early in 1963 we tried pair trawling for sprats up the Firth - our neighbour was the *Crimond*. Now this was a new thing and it happened to be a very profitable fishing, which lasted for three months. As it happened, that winter was a very bad winter and there were plenty of sprats up the Firth. Now after that we started the seine net again right into the end of July. Then the herring fishing started off Seahouses and went as far south as Whitby and Scarborough, so with doing so well catching sprats at the pair trawling, we thought we would have a go at the herring - Bill Boyter of the Crimond and me. So we left a good fishing at the seine net and went away to try the herring trawl but we just couldn't get moving for foreigners. The fishing would have done right enough but there were that many boats we just couldn't get moved. This is confirmed by a newspaper cutting that was in the *Daily Express* and there was a photograph showing a Russian trawler towing, close along side of us as we were hauling the net. But this fishing just didn't really do because we just didn't have the power to catch the herring.

After all this came the salmon fishing the following year. Now this turned out to be a great fishing. The nets were 150 yards long and 60 mashes deep. The mash was from five and a quarter inches to five and three quarter inches. Now you'll realise that these nets were floating on the surface and you'll realise how near the surface the salmon swims. They were nylon nets which were very fine. We had twenty nets which we shot in two fleets often. The reason for this was that if you shot all twenty it put too much of a strain on the nets and, with having only the one rape that we called the cork rape, were awfy easy rolled up so we had to shoot them in two fleets. The fishing was mostly done in the dark and we had lighted buoys on each end of each fleet, what we called a winkie. Now we shot both fleets end for end. We didn't lie fast to the nets like you did at the drift nets as I said before, because they would roll up if you put a strain on the nets. Now we shot the two fleets end for end and we just lay at the end of the fleet watching the boats to see that they kept clear of your net. The start of this fishing was off Berwick so we had to keep five miles off the shore as the Tweed river board claimed up to five miles off, so we had to keep outside of that but there were plenty fish from there to as far as twelve miles off. We would shoot away as far as the five mile line and we would draw it out on the chart. The two fleets we shot across the tide, but as we were bothered a lot by seals taking the fish we would haul our nets often - every hour. So we would haul the inmost fleet first, then after it was hauled just run along the fleet and whenever we got to the end of the fleet we dropped a winkie and shot the fleet that you had just hauled. Now we did this all night and there was one night we finished up as far as twelve miles off and that was our best haul that night - we got ten big fish. That was a good shot in itself as they were worth about £5 the piece. Anybody that's been to the salmon fishing realises the damage that is done by seals. In fact we had to buy a shotgun to try and scare them away. Now during this time we were fishing off Berwick we heard of two boats with good shots off Girdleness, so we went north because we knew we wouldn't be bothered so much by the seals. Our first shot, which we shot five miles off Girdleness, was the best shot we had while we were at the salmon. We got sixty one fish and I believe we would have got more, but they were aye saying "we'll need to watch, if seals get among them, they'll clean us out". So we hauled and we got sixty one but there were no seals there. As the fishing went on we went farther north. We shot off Buckie one night and we got a good enough shot but of course this fishing was no use in calm weather. You just didn't get anything, it had to be a fresh wind.

At the finish we were working as far north as Tarbetness. Then it was too good weather. The good weather was coming in and you would maybe get one night or two nights with a fresh kind of wind.and that was the only nights you got any fish, so we decided to go back to the seine net again. I would like to mention that we were at it a fortnight during the summer, in the month of July - during daylight we were fishing at that time, and we just shot the same way, two fleets on end and you used to see the fish hitting the net. With it being through the day we used to go up along the nets and just put her bow to and lift - get a hold of the rape and just lift the fish aboard and take the fish out and let the net go again. I have seen us lying the whole day without hauling the nets. This method of salmon fishing was stopped by an Act of Parliament during that same year.

Appendix VIII:
Fishing Methods referred to in the Maritime Tables

Motor Trawl: The gear consists of a net in the shape of a funnel attached to the vessel by wire ropes or "warps". As the net is towed over the sea floor the mouth is kept open by a combination of boards, floats and weights. The tail end of the net where the fish are trapped is know as the 'Cod End'. The length of the warps is normally about 3.5 to 4 times the depth of the water and can extend in depths of 110 metres to about 450 metres from the stern of the vessel. This method is used by the deep sea trawlers operating mainly out of Aberdeen. Other single-vessel trawling methods (Industrial Trawl, Light Trawl and *Nephrop Trawl) follow the same principles. Light Trawl and *Nephrop Trawl are used by 'Inshore' vessels in the 10 metre to 25 metre group, many of which are multi-purpose and may also use seine nets.

Two-Boat Trawl: ('Pair Trawl', 'Mid-Water Trawl'). A variant of trawling used to fish at intermediate depths between the surface and the sea floor. The net is towed by two vessels which may be up to 400 metres apart, the depth of the net being mainly controlled by the length of the warps and the vessels' speed, used by vessels in the inshore fleet for catching both demersal and pelagic species.

Seine Net: Another bottom fishing method. The gear consists of a sac of netting with wings on either side, kept in position vertically by floats and weights. Long warps are attached to the net, one of which is initially fastened to a flag pole passed through a 'dahn' buoy. The vessel steams forward paying out warp, then the net itself, then more warp to form a rough triangle back to the dahn, which may be some 1 - 3 kilometres distant from the net. The vessel then steams ahead, causing the warps to herd the fish into the path of the net, which is finally winched aboard.

Beam Trawl: The beam trawl is a bottom fishing trawl net, used for catching flatfish with the headrope attached to a beam towed along the bottom on runners at either end. The net is heavily weighted with chain on the underside and has trickler chains running in front when fishing.

*A 'Nephrop', otherwise known as a 'Norway Lobster', is the type of shellfish landed at Pittenweem which is referred to as a 'Prawn'.

A yawl being rowed into Anstruther harbour past the Hannah Harvey lighthouse. Half way up the photograph on the right hand side the coffer dam preventing water from entering the Inner Harbour during the construction of 'The Folly' can be seen.

Crail fishermen Tam Meldrum (left) and Robert Murray (White Cap)

Acknowledgements

I seem to be fated to write about things, which although they may not have completely died out are maybe just about to. Take, for example, the way in which our language has changed over the years. In looking through my notebooks I came across a copy of a letter Robert Louis Stevenson had sent to his father:

"and so I trudge to the pier again e'er I can go further with my noble design. I had a ride today on B's pony. He gave me rather a dismal account of its temper, mouth etc. M told me I must not believe it all, for B was not a very daring horseman, he thought. His own groom was more explicit". "Has Mr. B. a good seat" I asked. "Him, heck no, by God, he's a puir show in the saddle, him".

Notice the pronoun underlined. Typical of the East Neuk of yesteryear. I heard it last when Tammy Robertson came and stood beside my wife and I as we spoke to two girls, Senior Pupils of the Waid Academy. On their departure, Tammy said, "They're twa fine lassies, they". I have also heard it while at a school football match, when one spectator addressed another: "He's a braw player, him".

Here concludes the homily.

Now you will see from the lists of fishing boats in the three main fishing ports of the East Neuk, namely Anstruther, Pittenweem and St. Monans, how they have deteriorated since 1914. I will be well advised to make no comment, but instead I'll get on with thanking people who have helped me. Starting with St. Andrews - Dr. Malcolm lives there and has been helpful with photos, along with St. Andrews University Library, who have granted the use of photographs from the 'Cowie Collection'. I am also grateful to Christopher Rush, who loaned me George Bruce's book on St. Andrews. Crail now, where Alfred Smith got me more photos of Crail than I ever managed before. I must also thank John Murray, again for obtaining photographs.

At Anster and Cellardyke I would like to thank R. Gardner, A. Anderson

155

and John Doig, whose work on the photos is indispensable; T. Murray, T. Gardner, J. Mayes, W. Kinnear and A. Parker, who typed out the series of articles by Auld Wull from the East Fife Observer and the Scottish Fisheries Museum. Last, but not least, I would like to thank Cellardyke born James Corstorphine, now a resident of Leven, for the many hours he has spent putting this book together.

Along to Pittenweem, where Billy Hughes of the Fishermen's Mutual Association, John Horsburgh, C. Bowman and A. Watson have all been a great help, not forgetting the tape recording from the late W. McBain.

In St. Monans now, some photos from the museum means thanks to R. Ovenstone and Ian Reekie; to boatbuilder R. Latto (a picture of whom may be seen in his own self-built boat), J. Dunn and to the skipper of the *Orion*, W. Scott.

As for Buckhaven, I must mention Frank Rankin, who supplied several photographs. Unfortunately I have been unable to obtain a photograph of the Buckhaven boat *Iris* ML345, although I am still working on it.

There are also four ladies I would like to mention: C. Keay, C. Kerr, M. Morrison and J. Pearson. Thanks to them all.

Peter Smith.